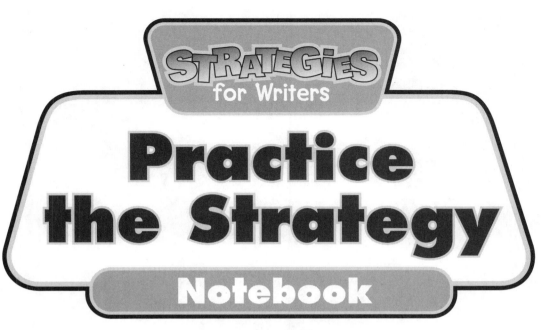

Practice the Strategy Notebook

Level F

Authors

Leslie W. Crawford, Ed.D.
Georgia College & State University

Rebecca Bowers Sipe, Ed.D.
Eastern Michigan University

Cover Design

Tommaso Design Group

Production by Laurel Tech Integrated Publishing Services

ISBN 0-7367-1248-8

Zaner-Bloser, Inc., P.O. Box 16764, Columbus, Ohio 43216-6764   (1-800-421-3018)

Printed in the United States of America

07 08 09 (106) 10 9 8

NARRATIVE
writing

EXPOSITORY
writing

PERSUASIVE
writing

DESCRIPTIVE
writing

EXPOSITORY

writing

TEST

writing

Prewriting

Gather

Pick an incident I saw. Take notes on what I saw and heard.

Just as Derek did, you will write notes about your personal experience and memory of an event that you have witnessed. Here are some sample notes on a girls' lacrosse game. The notes will be used to write an eyewitness account.

My Notes on the Blue Jays v. Comets Girls' Lacrosse Game

- Nina: my sister, attacker—plays for the Blue Jays, South High School girls' lacrosse team.

- Blue Jays v. Comets: Jays won 7 to 6.

- big upset of last season

- Comets were undefeated before that game.

- last minutes of game: Nina scores twice.

- 1st time: Nina gets a pass from the side, somebody checks her (taps her stick) to get the ball, she does a turn and then shoots overhead from midfield.

- Everybody goes wild when Nina scores.

- 2nd time: Comet's bad pass misses, Nina gets the ball and goes straight for the goal and scores.

Prewriting

Gather

Pick an incident I saw. Take notes on what I saw and heard.

your own writing

Now it's your turn to practice this strategy with a different topic. On the lines below, jot down facts and details about an event that you have watched. For example, maybe you saw an air show, a parade, a hot air balloon event, or a concert. Draw from your personal experience and memory.

_____

_____

_____

_____

_____

_____

_____

_____

_____

_____

_____

_____

_____

_____

Now go back to Derek's work on page 19 in the Student Edition.

Prewriting

Organize
Use my notes to make a 5 W's chart.

Here's how one writer used a 5 W's chart to organize the notes on page 6.

What happened?	• Blue Jays win lacrosse game with Comets—big upset.
	• Comets had been undefeated.
	• Nina scores 1st time with overhead shot from midfield.
	• Nina gets bad pass and scores again.
Who was there?	• Nina and other Blue Jays
	• Comets
	• fans for both teams
Why did it happen?	• Nina is an attacker!
	• She scored twice in last minutes of game.
When did it happen?	• last season
Where did it happen?	• South High School field

Prewriting

Organize
Use my notes to make a
5 W's chart.

your own
writing

Now it's time for you to practice this strategy. Use this 5 W's chart to organize your notes on the event that you saw.

What happened?	
Who was there?	
Why did it happen?	
When did it happen?	
Where did it happen?	

RETURN
Now go back to Derek's work on page 20 in the Student Edition.

Drafting

Write
Draft my account. Put the most important of the 5 W's in the lead paragraph.

Now it's time for you to practice this strategy. Read this lead paragraph below from an eyewitness account of the girls' lacrosse game.

> My sister Nina is an attacker! She plays an attack position on our high school girls' lacrosse team, the Blue Jays. I watched Nina show her stuff against the Comets on their home field last season. The Comets were undefeated until that game.

Now identify any 5 W's in the paragraph.

Who: _____

What: _____

_____

When: _____

Where: _____

Why: _____

_____

Drafting

Write

Draft my account. Put the most important of the 5 W's in the lead paragraph.

your own writing

Now it's time for you to practice this strategy. Review the 5 W's chart you made on page 9. Then write a lead paragraph that includes what you think are the most important of those 5 W's for your event. Circle the words that address the 5 W's you included. Label each circle to indicate which of the 5 W's it is. Then continue writing your draft. Use another sheet of paper, if necessary.

_____

_____

_____

_____

_____

_____

_____

_____

_____

_____

_____

_____

RETURN Now go back to Derek's work on page 22 in the Student Edition.

ReVising

Elaborate

Make the story more lively by varying sentence beginnings.

Using variety in your sentence beginnings makes your writing more interesting. Here are four ways to begin a sentence:

Subject: **Lacrosse sticks** are called crosses.
She yelled encouragement to her teammates.

Adverb: **Quickly,** she turned.
Painfully, she got up and limped to the sidelines.

Phrase: **Swinging her crosse,** she launched the ball.
After the game, everyone relaxed.

Dependent Clause: **When the whistle blew,** the game started.
If Nina sees an opportunity, she will take it.

On the line following each sentence below, write **S** for sentences that begin with a subject. Write **A** for those that begin with an adverb, **P** for those that begin with a phrase, and **DC** for the one dependent clause.

1. A lacrosse ball is yellow and made of solid rubber. _____

2. The object of the game is to shoot the ball into the opponent's goal. _____

3. Straining to reach, she stretched out to catch the ball. _____

4. All players must wear mouth guards. _____

5. Determined to win, the team pumped up its energy. _____

6. Skillfully, she tapped the crosse and dislodged the ball. _____

7. Concentrating on the goal, she charged through the defense. _____

8. Patiently, the coach explained the play again. _____

9. A strike toward a player's head is a foul. _____

10. Running like a rabbit, she entered the goal circle. _____

11. A muddy field makes playing difficult. _____

12. Carefully, the athletic trainer wrapped the injured leg. _____

13. After the game was over, the parents congratulated their daughters on a fine game. _____

14. Proudly, Nina accepted the coach's compliment. _____

ReVising

Elaborate   Make the story more lively by varying sentence beginnings.

Now it's time for you to practice this strategy. Rewrite the sentences below, using different beginnings. The first one is done for you.

I. The goalkeeper lunged to block the shot.

Lunging, the goalkeeper blocked the shot.

2. Nina jumped into the air and shouted.

_____

3. The players heard the whistle and stood still.

_____

4. The Comets dominated the field in the first half.

_____

5. She whipped the ball forcefully into the net.

_____

6. The center saw Nina downfield and passed her the ball.

_____

7. She dodged another player and quickly passed the ball.

_____

8. The players watched the scoreboard anxiously.

_____

9. She dropped the ball suddenly.

_____

10. The coach groaned as the Comets scored again.

_____

Remember: Use this strategy in **your own writing**

RETURN Now go back to Derek's work on page 23 in the Student Edition.

Narrative Writing • Eyewitness Account   **13**

ReVising

Clarify

Replace ordinary words or phrases with more interesting and colorful words.

Now it's time for you to practice this strategy. Above each of the ordinary words or groups of words underlined below, write a more colorful word from the Word Bank.

Word Bank

battle	warriors	training
field	chased	zoned
sport	participants	preparation
extended	created	braves
pursued	stretched	combat
contestants	contest	invented

Native Americans, came up with the game of lacrosse. The men played the game as a way to get ready for war. Thousands of players carrying long sticks ran after a deerskin ball. The playing area went for miles.

Now provide your own colorful words for the ordinary words underlined in this paragraph.

A good goalkeeper is very important. Her job is to guard the goal. She should be brave and watchful. Above all, she should be able to stop a ball before it hits the net.

Now go back to Derek's work on page 24 in the Student Edition.

Remember: Use this strategy in **your own writing**

Editing

Proofread

Watch for sentence fragments. To avoid run-ons, check to see that all compound sentences are joined correctly.

⌐ Indent.

≡ Make a capital.

/ Make a small letter.

∧ Add something.

ℓ Take out something.

⊙ Add a period.

⌗ New paragraph

ⓢⓟ Spelling error

Now it's time for you to practice this strategy. Here is the revised draft of the eyewitness account. The writer probably made different word choices than you did in the second paragraph. Use the proofreading marks to correct any errors. Use a dictionary to help with spelling.

Nina the Attacker!

My sister Nina is an attacker! She plays an attack position on our high school girls' lacrosse team, the Blue Jays. I watched Nina show her stuff against the Comets last season. The Comets were undefeeted until that game.

With minutes left on the scoreboard, the Comets led 6 to 5. Then the blue Jays gained possession upfield. Swiftly, Nina cut and snagged a sidelong pass. A defender taped Nina's lacrosse stick to disloge the ball, it stayed put. Nina twisted away and dashed to an open spot midfield. Leaped into the air and hurled the ball over the astonished players into the net. The stands rocked with cheers

The Comets were choking with fury and acheing to score. On the next play, they lobbed a clummsy overhead pass. Nina intersepted it and I screamed, "Go! Go! Go!" Nina dodged defenders and rushed toward the goal.

the Comets' goalkeeper was like a caged lion. Behind her facemask, she growling. Nina pitched the ball into the goal and it flew past the lion. The Blue Jays conckered the Comets! Nina the Attacker rules!

↩ RETURN Now go back to Derek's work on page 26 in the Student Edition.

Remember: Use this strategy in **your own writing**

Using a Rubric

Use this rubric to evaluate Derek's eyewitness account on pages 27–29 in your Student Edition. You can work with a partner.

Audience

Is the first paragraph clear and interesting?

Organization

How well does the writer use the 5 W's (*who, what, when, where,* and *why*) to organize the story?

Elaboration

Does the writer make the story more lively by varying sentence beginnings?

Clarification

Does the writer use interesting and colorful words to make meanings clear?

your own writing

Save this rubric. Use it to check your own writing.

Conventions & Skills

Has the writer avoided sentence fragments and run-ons?

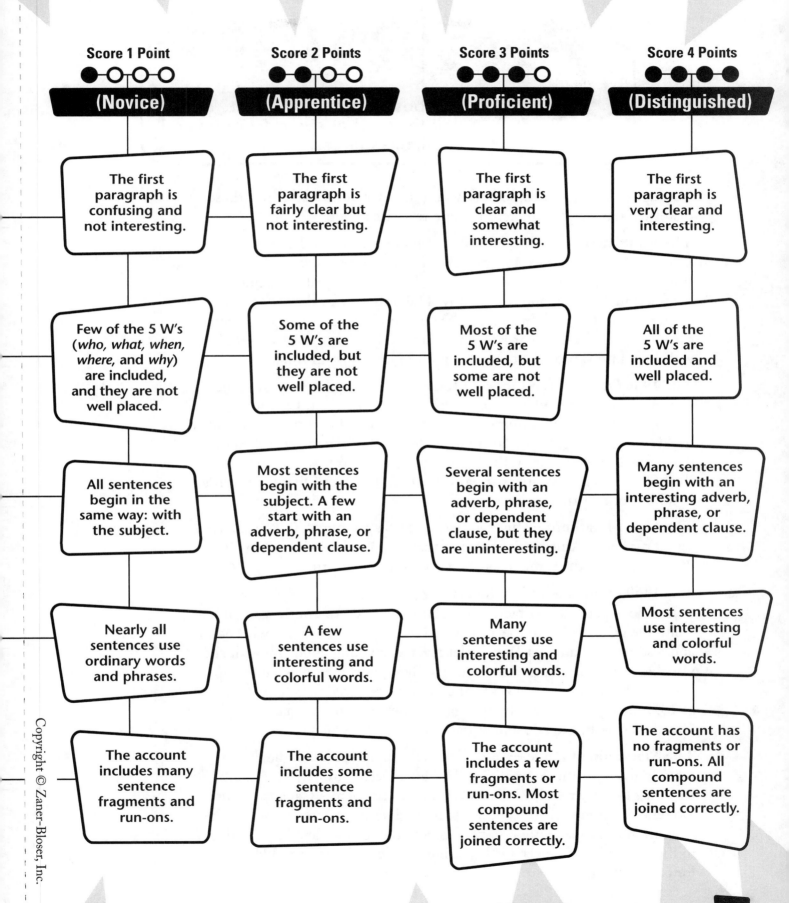

Score 1 Point
●○○○
(Novice)

Score 2 Points
●●○○
(Apprentice)

Score 3 Points
●●●○
(Proficient)

Score 4 Points
●●●●
(Distinguished)

The first paragraph is confusing and not interesting.

The first paragraph is fairly clear but not interesting.

The first paragraph is clear and somewhat interesting.

The first paragraph is very clear and interesting.

Few of the 5 W's (*who*, *what*, *when*, *where*, and *why*) are included, and they are not well placed.

Some of the 5 W's are included, but they are not well placed.

Most of the 5 W's are included, but some are not well placed.

All of the 5 W's are included and well placed.

All sentences begin in the same way: with the subject.

Most sentences begin with the subject. A few start with an adverb, phrase, or dependent clause.

Several sentences begin with an adverb, phrase, or dependent clause, but they are uninteresting.

Many sentences begin with an interesting adverb, phrase, or dependent clause.

Nearly all sentences use ordinary words and phrases.

A few sentences use interesting and colorful words.

Many sentences use interesting and colorful words.

Most sentences use interesting and colorful words.

The account includes many sentence fragments and run-ons.

The account includes some sentence fragments and run-ons.

The account includes a few fragments or run-ons. Most compound sentences are joined correctly.

The account has no fragments or run-ons. All compound sentences are joined correctly.

PrewRitiNg

Gather

Choose a historical event. Take notes on that event from several reliable sources.

Throughout history, people have run in many races. Read about these historical races and runners. Pick one to write about.

The First Iditarod—One of the most famous races in the world, the Iditarod, began as a race for life. In 1925, a disease called diphtheria threatened the town of Nome, Alaska. The shipment of medicine was stranded in Nenana, 660 miles away. The only way to deliver the life-saving medication was by dog sled. Many mushers and their dog teams came out to help. Gunnar Kasson's team led by Balto, the heroic half-wolf half-husky, brought the medicine to Nome just in time.

The 1936 Olympics and Jesse Owens—Jesse Owens is a sports super-star. As a member of the 1936 American Track & Field Olympic Team, he was the first American in the history of Olympic Track and Field to win four gold medals in a single day. Jesse won the 100-meter dash, the 200-meter dash, the broad jump, and was a key member of the 400-meter relay team that won the gold. Jesse set Olympic records in all but one of these events.

The First Marathon—After the Battle of Marathon in 490 BC, the Greeks sent a runner to Athens with news of their victory. The winner ran about 26 miles; this is the same distance modern marathon runners run today.

The 1960 Olympics and Wilma Rudolph—Wilma Rudolph overcame tremendous personal obstacles to become the first American woman to win three gold medals in the 1960 Olympics. Wilma was born with polio and also had pneumonia and scarlet fever as a young child. Though she was told she would never walk, with family support and physical therapy, she was able to walk by age 11. She became involved in school sports at 13. During the 1960 Olympic games she won gold medals in the 100-meter dash, the 200-meter dash, and the 400-meter relay.

The Marathon of Hope—Terry Fox was a sportsman who didn't run for medals or for the competition. He ran a race of awareness. After he lost a leg to cancer in 1977, Terry decided to run across Canada to raise awareness and money for cancer research. His run became known as the Marathon of Hope. Although he was not able to complete his race due to the return of his cancer, his Marathon of Hope raised over $24 million for cancer research.

PReWRitiNg

Gather

Choose a historical event. Take notes on that event from several reliable sources.

your own writing

Now it's time for you to practice this strategy. On the lines below, jot down facts and details about the event you chose on page 18. Look it up in an encyclopedia first to get an overview. Then check other reliable sources.

_____

_____

_____

_____

_____

_____

_____

_____

_____

_____

_____

_____

_____

_____

_____

_____

_____

RETURN Now go back to Lauren's work on page 43 in the Student Edition.

Prewriting

Organize

Organize my notes into a story map.

your own writing

Now it's time for you to practice this strategy. Use this story map to organize your notes on the historical event you chose.

Setting—Time:

Setting—Place:

Characters:

Problem:

Plot/Events:

Ending/Resolution:

Now go back to Lauren's work on page 44 in the Student Edition.

Drafting

Write
Draft my episode. Include a clear beginning, middle, and end. Keep the focus on the event.

Now it's your turn to practice this strategy. A student is writing a historical account of the first marathon. He now has a clear beginning, middle, and end, although only the first part of his draft is shown here. However, he is having trouble staying on the topic. Locate a sentence in each paragraph that is off the topic. Write those sentences on the lines.

Almost 2,500 years ago, a Greek runner ran 26 miles to announce the outcome of a battle that changed history. You might have read about this battle in a history book. Then he collapsed, dead from exaustion. His run was the first marathon.

Why did he run? The story begins on September 12, 490 B.C. The Greeks faced the Persians on the planes of Marathon. The Persians had 40,000 troops. Darius, the Persian king, hoped to rule the world with this army, which was the most feared in Asia. The greeks had 10,000 men. They were the citizen army of Athens, a greek city-state. Athens is still a city today. Callimachus, the Athens commander-in-chief, met with Miltiades, one of his top generals. We are doomed." Callimachus said.

"Miltiades" responded, "it is in your hands, Callimachus, to make the Athenians slaves or to set them free. If we give up, there will be mizerry. If we fight, we may win. Athens could become the most important of the Greek cities. Do you want Athenians to become Persian slaves or noble Greeks"? I would rather be a noble Greek, wouldn't you?

Callimachus was quiet for a long time. I bet he was thinking things over. Then he answered, "We must fight to defend our city and the future of all Greeks. Get the troops ready!

Misplaced sentences:

Paragraph 1: _____

Paragraph 2: _____

Paragraph 3: _____

Paragraph 4: _____

Drafting

Write

Draft my episode. Include a clear beginning, middle, and end. Keep the focus on the event.

your own writing

Now it's your turn to practice this strategy. Write your own draft of the historical episode you chose. Refer to your story map on page 20 to make sure your account has a clear beginning, middle, and end. Remember to stay on the topic!

_____

_____

_____

_____

_____

_____

_____

_____

_____

_____

_____

_____

_____

_____

_____

Drafting

Write
Draft my episode. Include a clear beginning, middle, and end. Keep the focus on the event.

Use this space to continue the draft of your historical episode.

_____

_____

_____

_____

_____

_____

_____

_____

_____

_____

_____

_____

_____

_____

_____

_____

 Now go back to Lauren's work on page 46 in the Student Edition.

Revising

Elaborate
Add details that create a clear picture of the historical period.

Now it's time for you to practice this strategy. Read the facts below about the Greeks and the Persians at the time of the Battle of Marathon. Put a checkmark in front of facts you think would help readers better understand the story of the first marathon.

☐ **1.** All Greek cities were independent city-states.

☐ **2.** Greeks built elaborate temples to many gods.

☐ **3.** Greek armies used a phalanx formation.

☐ **4.** Greek women were not allowed to take part in public life.

☐ **5.** Greek men and women lived in different parts of the house.

☐ **6.** Greek soldiers wore metal helmets, leg guards, and leather tunics and carried spears and bronze shields.

☐ **7.** Each Greek city honored a specific god with festivals and sports competitions.

☐ **8.** Most Persians lived in poverty and were treated as slaves.

☐ **9.** Persians had huge birthday celebrations.

☐ **10.** The Persian army was the most feared in Asia.

☐ **11.** Persian soldiers wore bright uniforms and carried a woven shield and many different weapons.

☐ **12.** Persians had a special reverence for rivers.

☐ **13.** Persian rulers were the first to want to conquer the world.

☐ **14.** As a greeting, Persians kissed on the mouth or cheek, depending on rank.

☐ **15.** Persia was ruled by King Darius.

Remember: Use this strategy in *your own writing*

Now go back to Lauren's work on page 47 in the Student Edition.

ReVising

Clarify

Put the sentences in logical order so the story is easy to follow.

Now it's time for you to practice this strategy. Here is part of the third draft of the story of the first marathon. Read each paragraph and rearrange the sentences so they are in logical order. (Fix any other errors you find or wait until you edit.)

The Greek general Miltiades had a plan. He used only two or three rows of soldiers in the middle of the line. Seeing the weak middle, the Persians pushed toward it. Suddenly, they found themselves trapped by the soliders in the wings. Within a few hours, the Athenians had won a miraculelous victory—even though they were outnumbered four to one. On the wings, the rows were five or six soldiers deep.

The victory by Greece had long-reaching effects. If the Persians had won, our culture might be much different today. Greek culture floor-ished and spread. It became the foundation for civilizations in Europe and the United States.

The Greek festivals led to the first Olympic games in 1896. Those games included a long-distance race. It was about 26 miles—the distance from marathon to Athens. The battle had another effect, too.

Remember: Use this strategy in **your own writing**

 Now go back to Lauren's work on page 48 in the Student Edition

Editing
Proofread
Check to see that quotations are punctuated correctly.

Indent.
Make a capital.
Make a small letter.
Add something.
Take out something.
Add a period.
New paragraph
Spelling error

Now it's time for you to practice this strategy. Here is the draft of the historical episode about the first marathon. Use the proofreading marks to correct any errors. Use a dictionary to help with spelling.

The First Marathon

Almost 2,500 years ago, a Greek runner ran 26 miles to announce the outcome of a battle that changed history. Then he collapsed, dead from exaustion. His run was the first marathon.

Why did he run? The story begins on September 12, 490 B.C. The Greeks faced the Persians on the planes of Marathon. The Persians had 40,000 troops. Darius, the Persian king, hoped to rule the world with this army, which was the most feared in Asia. The Greeks had 10,000 men. They were the citizen army of Athens, a Greek city-state. Callimachus, the Athens commander-in-chief, met with Miltiades, one of his top generals. We are doomed." Callimachus said.

"Miltiades "responded, "it is in your hands, Callimachus, to make the Athenians slaves or to set them free. If we give up, there will be mizerry. If we fight, we may win. Athens could become the most important of the Greek cities. Do you want Athenians to become Persian slaves or noble Greeks"?

Callimachus was quiet for a long time. Then he answered, "We must fight to defend our city and the future of all Greeks. Get the troops ready!

In a surprise attack, the brave Greeks charged the Persians. The Greeks used a phalanx formation: rows of solders marched forward together with their spears sticking straight out.

Editing

Proofread

Check to see that quotations are punctuated correctly.

⌐ Indent.
≡ Make a capital.
/ Make a small letter.
∧ Add something.
ℓ Take out something.
⊙ Add a period.
New paragraph
(SP) Spelling error

The Greek general Miltiades had a plan. He used only two or three rows of soldiers in the middle of the line. On the wings, the rows were five or six soldiers deep. Seeing the weak middle, the Persians pushed toward it. Suddenly, they found themselves trapped by the soldiers in the wings. Within a few hours, the Athenians had won a miraculelous victory—even though they were outnumbered four to one.

Before the battle, Athens had sent a runner named Phidippedes 140 miles to Sparta, another Greek city-state, to ask for help. Sparta knew the Persians were a thret to all Greeks. Still, when Phidippedes returned to Athens, he said "A Spartan festival is going on. They cannot help us fight, but I can After his long run, Phidippedes fought in the Battle of Marathon. After the battle, a runner was sent to Athens with the astonishing news of victory. That runner, who died of exaustion, was probably Phidippedes.

The victory by Greece had long-reaching effects. Greek culture floorished and spread. It became the foundation for civilizations in Europe and the United States. If the Persians had won, our culture might be much different today.

The battle had another effect, too. Greek festivals led to the first Olympics in 1896. Those games included a long-distance race. It was about 26 miles—the distance from marathon to Athens.

Many cities have marathons today. The runners are tired afterwards, so it's a good thing they don't have to fight a historic battle on the same day!

Remember: Use this strategy in **your own writing**

RETURN Now go back to Lauren's work on page 50 in the Student Edition

Using a Rubric

Use this rubric to evaluate Lauren's work on pages 51–53 in the Student Edition. You can work with a partner.

How well does the writer introduce the historic event to the audience?

Does the story have a clear beginning, middle, and end? Does it stay focused on the event?

How well does the writer use descriptive details to create a clear picture of the historic period?

Does the writer put the sentences in a logical order?

your own writing

Save this rubric. Use it to check your own writing.

Are quotations punctuated correctly?

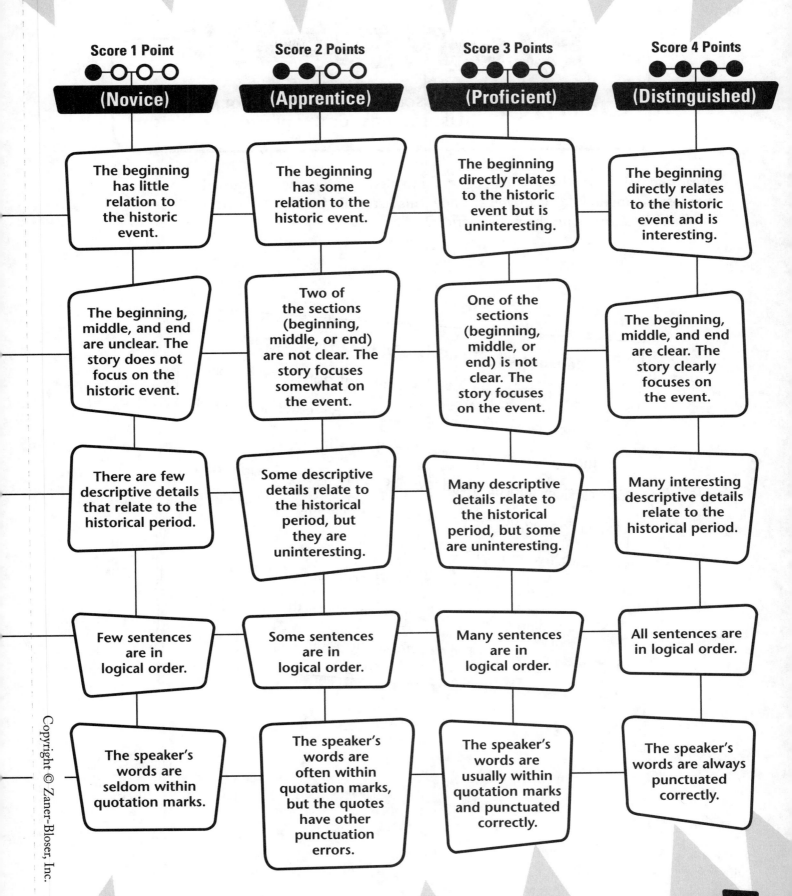

Score 1 Point	Score 2 Points	Score 3 Points	Score 4 Points
(Novice)	**(Apprentice)**	**(Proficient)**	**(Distinguished)**
The beginning has little relation to the historic event.	The beginning has some relation to the historic event.	The beginning directly relates to the historic event but is uninteresting.	The beginning directly relates to the historic event and is interesting.
The beginning, middle, and end are unclear. The story does not focus on the historic event.	Two of the sections (beginning, middle, or end) are not clear. The story focuses somewhat on the event.	One of the sections (beginning, middle, or end) is not clear. The story focuses on the event.	The beginning, middle, and end are clear. The story clearly focuses on the event.
There are few descriptive details that relate to the historical period.	Some descriptive details relate to the historical period, but they are uninteresting.	Many descriptive details relate to the historical period, but some are uninteresting.	Many interesting descriptive details relate to the historical period.
Few sentences are in logical order.	Some sentences are in logical order.	Many sentences are in logical order.	All sentences are in logical order.
The speaker's words are seldom within quotation marks.	The speaker's words are often within quotation marks, but the quotes have other punctuation errors.	The speaker's words are usually within quotation marks and punctuated correctly.	The speaker's words are always punctuated correctly.

Prewriting

Gather
Pick something to praise or criticize.
List reasons for my praise or criticism.

Read these reasons why a writer is grateful to a police officer who returned her lost mountain bike. Can you see how this list could be used to write a business letter praising the police officer?

Reasons Why I'm Grateful to Officer Juarez

- This is the second bike of mine that got stolen or lost.
- My new mountain bike is a cool purple color with a bell that glows in the dark. I really like it.
- Officer Juarez found my bike in the park one night and called me the very next day to let me know he had it. He didn't want me to worry about it.
- He met me on his day off and made sure I got my bike!
- Grandma gave me that bike for my birthday last year.
- He praised me for registering my bike.

Prewriting

Gather
Pick something to praise or criticize.
List reasons for my praise or criticism.

your own writing

Now it's your turn to practice this strategy. Pick something you would like to praise or criticize, such as a commercial, television show, restaurant, or product. You might also choose a person—but for praise only, please. List reasons for your praise or criticism on the lines below.

_____

_____

_____

_____

_____

_____

_____

_____

_____

_____

_____

_____

_____

_____

 Now go back to Jesse's work on page 65 in the Student Edition.

Prewriting

Organize

Organize my reasons from most important to least important.

Here is how one writer organized the reasons on page 30 in an order-of-importance organizer.

This is the second bike of mine that got stolen or lost.

Officer J found my bike and called me the very next day.

He met me on his day off and and made sure I got my bike.

He praised me for registering my bike.

My bike is purple with a bell that glows.

Grandma gave me that bike.

Expository Writing • Business Letter

Prewriting

Organize
Organize my reasons from most important to least important.

your own writing

Now it's time for you to practice this strategy. Use this order-of-importance organizer for your list of reasons. Write your reasons on the lines.

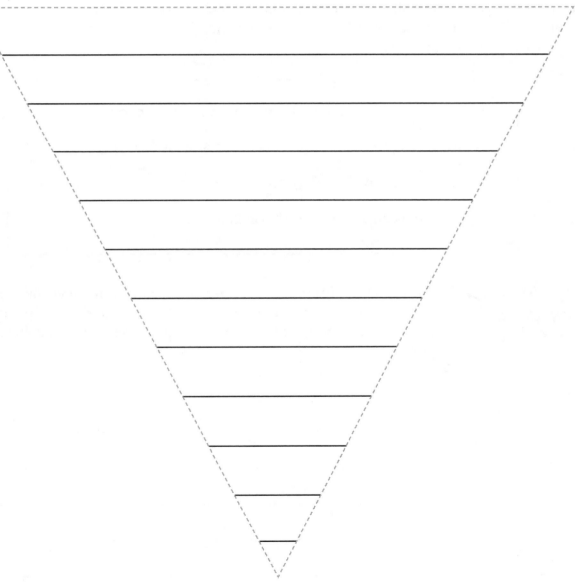

RETURN
Now go back to Jesse's work on page 66 in the Student Edition.

Drafting

Write
Draft my letter. State my purpose for writing in the first paragraph.

In a business letter, you should explain your purpose for writing in the first paragraph. Business people are busy and want to know the purpose of your letter right away.

Here is the first paragraph of the letter about the bike. Underline the sentence that explains the writer's purpose for writing. You may correct any errors you see now or later.

> Did you ever loose you're bike when you were a boy? If so,
>
> you now how I felt. I thought I'd never see my bike again.
>
> Thanks to you, tho, I got my bike back real fast. I wanted to
>
> tell you how much I apreciate your help.

your own writing

Now it's time for you to practice this strategy. Review your order-of-importance organizer on page 33. Then write the first paragraph of your business letter below. Underline the sentence that states your purpose.

_____

_____

_____

_____

_____

_____

RETURN Now go back to Jesse's work on page 68 in the Student Edition.

ReVising

Elaborate
Make sure I include all the necessary information.

Now it's time for you to practice this strategy. Read this paragraph from the letter to the police officer. Decide which of the information listed below would be important to add. Place a checkmark in front of the information you think should be included. Then use the lines to explain why you would put that information in the letter.

> My first bike was stolen last year and never recovered. this bike might have gotten stolen, too, after I accidentally left it at the park. Two stolen bikes in one year would have been too much for me too handle.

_____ **1.** the date when the first bike was stolen

_____ **2.** the place where his first bike was stolen

_____ **3.** the color of his first bike

_____ **4.** the date when he accidentally left his second bike at the park

_____ **5.** the name of the park where he left his bike

_____ **6.** who gave him his second bike

_____

_____

_____

_____

Remember:
Use this strategy in
your own writing

 Now go back to Jesse's work on page 69 in the Student Edition.

Revising

Clarify

Remember to restate my purpose for writing in my last paragraph. Check to see that I have used a businesslike tone.

The purpose for writing is so important in a business letter that you should state it again in your last paragraph. You saw how Jesse did that. Here's how the person writing about the lost bike did it. Underline the sentence that restates her purpose. (Correct any errors you see now, or wait until later.)

> You praised me for registering my bike but its you who
>
> deserves the praise. Some people wouldn't go out of they're
>
> way to return a lost bike promply. Because you did, I have my
>
> bike back. Thank you for careing.

your own writing

Now it's time for you to practice this strategy. Now write a concluding paragraph for your letter. Underline the sentence that restates your purpose for writing.

_____

_____

_____

_____

_____

_____

ReVising

Clarify

Remember to restate my purpose for writing in my last paragraph. Check to see that I have used a businesslike tone.

Now it's time for you to practice this strategy. Rewrite this paragraph. Replace the underlined words and phrases with ones that are more businesslike. Use the Word Bank or write in words of your own.

Word Bank

phoned me	surprised
unlikely to be found	disappointed
called me	shocked
missing for good	upset
contacted me	worried
lost forever	amazed

When you rang me up about my lost bike, I was totally freaked. I thought it was a goner. I was so bummed.

_____

_____

_____

_____

_____

_____

_____

Remember: Use this strategy in **your own writing**

RETURN Now go back to Jesse's work on page 70 in the Student Edition.

Editing

⊐ Indent.	ℓ Take out something.
☰ Make a capital.	⊙ Add a period.
/ Make a small letter.	⌗ New paragraph
∧ Add something.	SP Spelling error

Proofread

Check to see that all six parts of a business letter are included. Make sure homophones are used correctly.

Now it's time for you to practice this strategy. Here is the revised draft of the letter about the lost bicycle. Use the proofreading marks to correct any errors. Use a dictionary to help with spelling.

Anita James
148 W. Teale Court
Vernon, TX 76384
August 12, 20--

Gilbert Juarez
Police Officer
Vernon Police Department
1800 Cumberland Street
Vernon, TX 76384

Officer Juarez

   Did you ever lose you're bike when you were a boy? If so, you know how I felt when I couldn't find mine. I thought I'd never see it again. Thanks to you, tho, I got my bike back real fast. I want to tell you how much I apreciate your help.

   My first bike was stolen last year and never recovered. this bike might have gotten stolen, too, after I accidentally left it at the park. Two stolen bikes in one year would have been too much for me too handle.

Editing

⊐ Indent.	ℓ Take out something.
≡ Make a capital.	⊙ Add a period.
/ Make a small letter.	⌗ New paragraph
∧ Add something.	ⓈⓅ Spelling error

Proofread

Check to see that all six parts of a business letter are included. Make sure homophones are used correctly.

You said that it's probably because of it's glowing bell that you saw my bike in the park that night. Whose going to stop and investigate a little glow? You did You didn't know whose bike it was, but you checked the registration records immeediately and found out the bike was registered to me.

You called me the next day to tell me you found my bike, so I wouldn't be to worried. Then you met me at the police station on your day off especialy to return my bike.

You praised me for registering my bike but its you who deserves the praise. Some people wouldn't go out of they're way to return a lost bike promply. Because you did, I have my bike back. Thanks you for careing.

Sincereley,

Anita James

Remember:
Use this strategy in
your own writing

Now go back to Jesse's work on page 72 in the Student Edition.

Using a Rubric

Use this rubric to score Jesse's business letter on page 73 in your Student Edition. You can work with a partner.

Audience

Does the letter have a businesslike tone?

Organization

Are the points in the letter organized in order of importance?

Elaboration

Does the writer include all the necessary information?

Clarification

Is the purpose for writing stated in the first paragraph and restated in the concluding paragraph?

your own writing

Save this rubric. Use it to check your own writing.

Conventions & Skills

Are all six parts of a business letter included? Are homophones used correctly?

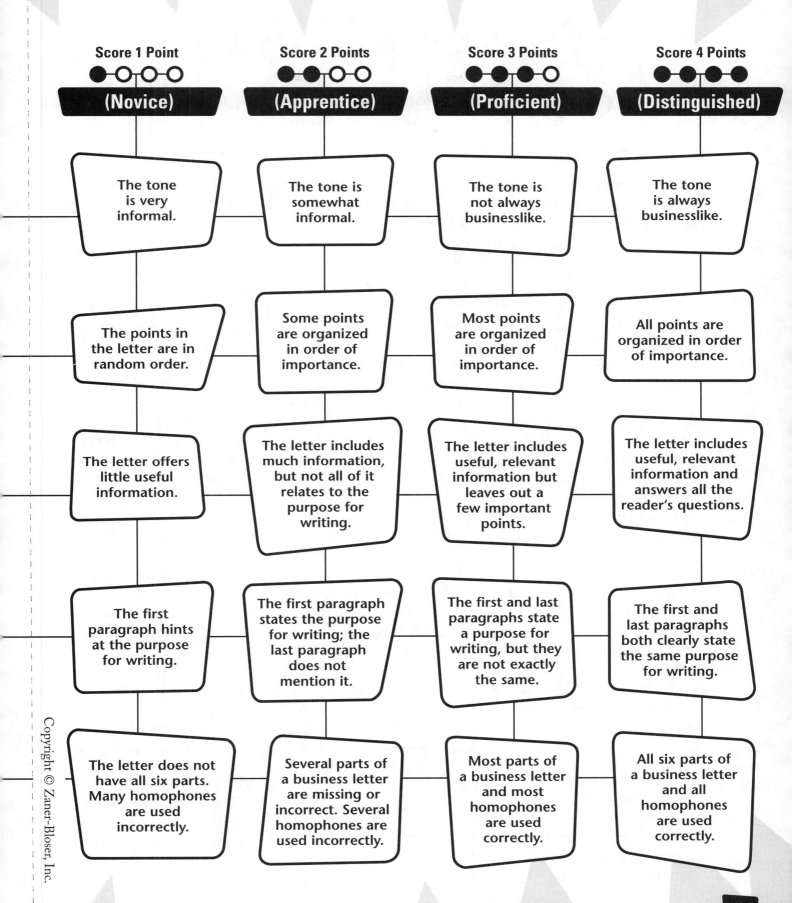

(Novice)   **(Apprentice)**   **(Proficient)**   **(Distinguished)**

The tone is very informal.

The tone is somewhat informal.

The tone is not always businesslike.

The tone is always businesslike.

The points in the letter are in random order.

Some points are organized in order of importance.

Most points are organized in order of importance.

All points are organized in order of importance.

The letter offers little useful information.

The letter includes much information, but not all of it relates to the purpose for writing.

The letter includes useful, relevant information but leaves out a few important points.

The letter includes useful, relevant information and answers all the reader's questions.

The first paragraph hints at the purpose for writing.

The first paragraph states the purpose for writing; the last paragraph does not mention it.

The first and last paragraphs state a purpose for writing, but they are not exactly the same.

The first and last paragraphs both clearly state the same purpose for writing.

The letter does not have all six parts. Many homophones are used incorrectly.

Several parts of a business letter are missing or incorrect. Several homophones are used incorrectly.

Most parts of a business letter and most homophones are used correctly.

All six parts of a business letter and all homophones are used correctly.

Prewriting

Gather
Read an article and take notes on the main points.

Now it's your turn to practice this strategy with a different topic. Read the article about skunks on this page and the next page. Identify the main points in the article by underlining them.

SKUNKS!
Could we help these little stinkers?
by DAVID SLOAN

"Did you say *six* baby skunks?" I said into the telephone.

"Yes," the caller said. While walking near a housing development, the caller had seen six baby skunks that appeared to be orphaned.

I climbed into my truck and drove to where the caller had seen the skunks. Sure enough, in the empty field there were six baby skunks.

I was working for the Kentucky Department of Fish and Wildlife. As a summer conservation officer, I dealt with many interesting situations involving animals. But I could tell that this one was going to stand out from the rest.

Orphans

Mother skunks are protective of their young, but there was no mother in sight. Skunks are usually nocturnal (nock-TURR-null), only coming out at night. But

these youngsters were moving about in broad daylight. It was obvious that they were orphans.

But what could a person do with them? They appeared to be four or five weeks of age. They were old enough to leave the den on their own, but were they old enough to take care of themselves? Looking at the tiny black-and-white figures, I doubted it.

I had been taught not to interfere with wild animals unless it was absolutely necessary. After some discussion, my coworkers and I agreed that the baby skunks needed limited help. Limited help means keeping an animal in the wild while giving some assistance.

But what should you feed six hungry baby skunks?

Skunks are omnivorous. Like us, they eat both meats and plants. But skunks eat some very different kinds of meats and plants than we do. Although they eat strawberries and apples, they also eat grasshoppers, frogs, bees, and mice. Not a very appealing diet to most of us!

A skunk's favorite food is grubs. These tiny insect larvae are like ice cream and cookies to a skunk. So with grubs in hand, we drove back to the vacant field.

These young skunks had no mother. Could they survive with a little help?

Warning!

The skunks seemed to pay little attention to us as we approached. This was probably because skunks can't see as well

Prewriting

Gather Read an article and take notes on the main points.

as we do. If you are more than four feet away from a skunk you are almost invisible to it.

But skunks are far from defenseless. If threatened, they have a very powerful spray that they can shoot out from their rear end. This liquid is stored in two grape-sized sacs under the skin below the tail. Skunks can accurately shoot this spray up to ten feet. And skunks are "fully loaded" and ready to spray by the time they're a month old.

We stood about twenty feet away and tossed grubs toward the skunks. The skunks seemed to have no idea there were grubs nearby. Unless we did something else, the skunks would starve, even though there was plenty of food.

With some reluctance, we moved closer until we were less than four feet away. The skunks "froze" as they stared at us. Their tails were pointing straight up. This is a skunk's first warning for intruders to beware. The next step would be to bend the tail

until it touches the back and to bend the body into a U-shape so that the rear end faces the intruder. This gets the skunk set for the next step: *Fire!*

Slowly we reached into the bag and pulled out some grubs. The skunks' tails seemed to twitch. Were they preparing to spray us? We tossed some grubs on the ground in front of them, and a few tails twitched again. But one brave skunk stepped forward. Soon the others did, too, and a feast was under way.

Wild, Not Mild

We had to be careful. We wanted to help the baby skunks survive, but we didn't want to tame them. If they became used to us, they would lose their fear of humans. Since they were living near a housing development, that would mean trouble. If these skunks began to raid garbage containers, make dens under houses, or stray into neighborhoods, they would have to be removed or destroyed. So our job was a tricky one.

One thing made the job a little easier. Skunks normally live in abandoned groundhog dens or other ready-made nesting places. They usually stay in a den for only a few weeks before moving on to another one. But since these skunks were without their mother, they continued living in the same den. We easily found the orphans each day, and they didn't roam into the housing development.

Over the next four weeks we gradually stopped feeding the skunks. If they were to survive in the wild, they would have to learn to find their own food. Soon the skunks stopped coming out in the daytime. They had become nocturnal.

A follow-up study showed that they had moved into the nearby woods.

In a way, I was sad to see them go, but I was also happy. They had made it. They were still wild creatures, and in a year or two would probably have young ones of their own. ■

Prewriting

Gather

Read an article and take notes on the main points.

Now that you have read the article, read the notes about it below. Three of these notes are not main points. Cross out those three.

Notes on "Skunks!

Could we help these little stinkers?"

- Six orphaned baby skunks found in empty field.

- Mother skunks are protective of their young.

- KY conservation officers helped but didn't want to make skunks tame.

- Can spray powerful liquid up to 10 feet.

- Spray stored in two grape-sized sacs under the tail.

- Skunks finally became nocturnal and took care of themselves.

- Skunks would some day have babies of their own.

PreWriting

Gather

Read an article and take notes on the main points.

your own writing

Now it's time for you to practice this strategy. Find an interesting article to summarize. It should be about as long as the one about the baby skunks. It can be from a magazine at home or in your library. You also could use a short section in a textbook. Read it and take notes below on the main ideas.

_____

_____

_____

_____

_____

_____

_____

_____

_____

_____

_____

_____

_____

_____

_____

_____

_____

_____

 Now go back to Eva's work on page 87 in the Student Edition.

PRewRitiNg

Organize Use my notes to make a spider map.

Now it's time for you to practice this strategy. Review the notes on page 44 from the article on baby skunks. Use them to fill in the spider map below.

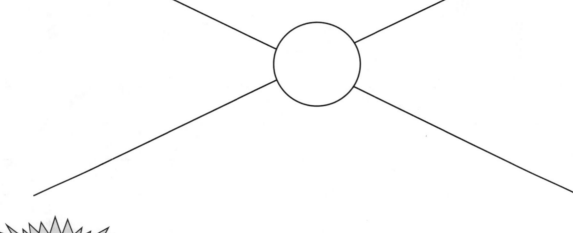

your own writing Now review your own notes on page 45. Use them to complete this spider map.

 Now go back to Eva's work on page 88 in the Student Edition.

Drafting

Write   Draft my summary. State the topic in the first sentence. Include all the main points from the article.

Now it's time for you to practice this strategy. You know that a summary should begin by stating the topic. Read these possible opening paragraphs for the summary about the baby skunks. Circle the paragraph that would make the best opening paragraph.

> Wild skunks are very difficult to help. You do not want to make them tame because then they will lose their fear of humans. They might begin raiding garbage cans and have to be removed or destroyed.

> Conservation workers in Kentucky found a way to help six abandoned baby skunks. They carefully fed them grubs until they were ready to survive on their own.

> Baby skunks, even abandoned ones, are not defenseless. They can shoot a powerful spray as far as ten feet. They can see only about four feet, so this can cause a problem.

Explain why you chose the paragraph you circled.

_____

_____

_____

_____

You can continue to practice the Write strategy on the next page.

Drafting

Write

Draft my summary. State the topic in the first sentence and include only the main points from the article.

your own writing

Now it's time for you to practice this strategy. Now use the notes from your main idea table to write a summary of the article you chose. You might want to review the article again to make sure you do not omit any of the main points.

_____

_____

_____

_____

_____

_____

_____

_____

_____

_____

_____

_____

_____

_____

Now go back to Eva's work on page 90 in the Student Edition.

Revising

Elaborate — Make sure I have included only important details.

Now it's time for you to practice this strategy. Read this part of a draft of the summary about the orphaned skunks. Cross out unnecessary details.

Summary of "Skunks! Could we help these little stinkers?"

Conservation workers in Kentucky helped six orphaned baby skunks found in an empty field near a housing development. Although skunks are nocturnal, the babies was out in daylight. The mother of the skunks were nowhere around, and the babies were two young to survive on there own. The workers guessed that they were four or five weeks old, old enough to leave their den, but not old enough to take care of themselves.

The workers knows it is best not to interfere too much with wildlife, so they offered the skunks limited help. They gave the skunks grubs—their favorite food. Skunks also eat strawberries, apples, grasshoppers, bees, mice, and frogs. At first, the workers attempted to feed them from a distance. They did not want the skunks to lose their fear of humans. Then they might wander into the housing development. They might get into people's garbage cans and make a mess. However, skunks sees poorly beyond four feet, so the workers finally had to drop the food close to the hungry orphans. Soon the baby skunks were eating the grubs.

Remember: Use this strategy in **your own writing**

Now go back to Eva's work on page 91 in the Student Edition.

ReVising

Clarify   Take out wordy phrases and sentences.

Now it's time for you to practice this strategy. The sentences below are all too wordy. Rewrite them, omitting any unnecessary words. The first sentence is rewritten for you.

1. Because skunks are nocturnal, they search for food to eat at night after it gets good and dark.

   Because skunks are nocturnal, they search for food at night.

2. They gobble up dog food and cat food and other pet food that has been left outside where they can get it and tear open the bags.

   _____

3. Skunks even make dens for themselves under houses and homes in which people live.

   _____

4. Conservation workers do not want skunks to become tame and used to people and not wild anymore.

   _____

5. The baby skunks would some day grow up and have babies or little ones of their own to take care of and feed.

   _____

6. Grubs are the most favorite food of all for skunks. They love grubs more than any other food.

   _____

7. Have you ever seen or observed a skunk in the neighborhood where you and your family live every day?

   _____

8. If a skunk's tail points straight up in the air, you should take notice and beware and be careful.

   _____

 Now go back to Eva's work on page 92 in the Student Edition.

 Remember: Use this strategy in **your own writing**

Editing

Proofread

⊐ Indent.	ℓ Take out something.
≡ Make a capital.	⊙ Add a period.
/ Make a small letter.	# New paragraph
∧ Add something.	SP Spelling error

Check to see that the subject and verb of each sentence agree.

Now it's time for you to practice this strategy. Here is the revised draft of the summary about the skunks. Use proofreading marks to correct errors. Use a dictionary to help with spelling.

Conservation workers in Kentucky helped six orphaned baby skunks found in an empty field near a housing development. Although skunks are nocturnal, the babies was out in daylight. The mother of the skunks were nowhere around, and the babies were two young to survive on there own.

The workers knows it is best not to interfere too much with wildlife, so they offered the skunks limited help. The workers gave the skunks grubs— their favorite food. At first, the workers attempted to feed them from a distance. They did not want the skunks to lose their fear of humans. Then they might wander into the housing development. However, skunks sees poorly beyond four feet, so the workers finally had to drop the food close to the hungry orphans. Soon the baby skunks were eating the grubs.

The workers were cautious. If a skunk feel thretened, it shoots a power-ful liquid from its rear end at the intruder. It can spray up to 10 feet.

Skunks in the wild usually migrates from den to den. Fortunately, these babies remained in one den, so it were easy for the workers to locate them every day. Over four weeks, the workers gradually stopped feeding the skunks. Soon the skunks became nocturnal and moved into the nearby woods.

Remember: Use this strategy in **your own writing**

 Now go back to Eva's work on page 94 in the Student Edition.

Using a Rubric

Use this rubric to evaluate Eva's summary on page 95 in your Student Edition. You can work with a partner.

Does the writer state the topic in the first sentence so the reader knows what the summary is about?

Does the writer organize the main points in a logical way?

Does the writer include only the important details?

Does the writer avoid using wordy phrases and sentences?

your own writing

Save this rubric. Use it to check your own writing.

Do the subject and verb of each sentence agree?

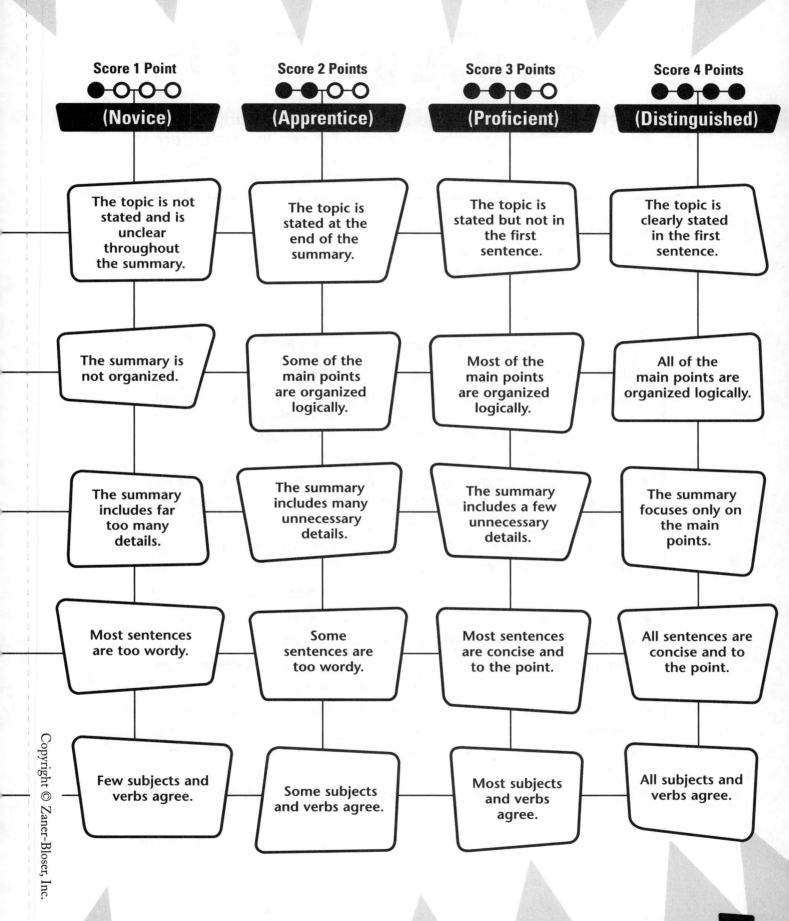

Score 1 Point
(Novice)

Score 2 Points
(Apprentice)

Score 3 Points
(Proficient)

Score 4 Points
(Distinguished)

The topic is not stated and is unclear throughout the summary.

The topic is stated at the end of the summary.

The topic is stated but not in the first sentence.

The topic is clearly stated in the first sentence.

The summary is not organized.

Some of the main points are organized logically.

Most of the main points are organized logically.

All of the main points are organized logically.

The summary includes far too many details.

The summary includes many unnecessary details.

The summary includes a few unnecessary details.

The summary focuses only on the main points.

Most sentences are too wordy.

Some sentences are too wordy.

Most sentences are concise and to the point.

All sentences are concise and to the point.

Few subjects and verbs agree.

Some subjects and verbs agree.

Most subjects and verbs agree.

All subjects and verbs agree.

Expository Writing • Summary

53

Prewriting

Gather

Think about a book I liked and find another book that is similar yet different. Jot notes about the first book. Keep a response journal as I read the new book.

Now it's time for you to practice this strategy with a different topic.
Have you read the novel *Catherine, Called Birdy* by Karen Cushman?
Here are one writer's notes about that book. Read the notes. Then read
the directions on the next page.

My Notes on Catherine, Called Birdy

- Diary of one year in life of girl in medieval England

- Catherine: 14 years old, called Birdy (keeps birds), daughter of rich manor lord. Birdy thinks father "conspires to sell me like a cheese to some lack-wit seeking a wife"; describes herself as "stubborn, peevish, and prickly as a thistle."

- Father is mean and greedy; mother is sweet. They think Catherine's duty is to obey her father and learn to be a lady. "Hemming and mending and fishing for husbands" are her life.

- Catherine is always plotting how she can escape the "prison" of the castle and not have to marry someone she doesn't love.

- Her friend is Perkin, the goat boy; she teaches him to read.

- Life is uncomfortable: she shares bed with fleas, makes gross herbal medicines, can't bathe all winter (too cold).

- She handles serious problem of arranged marriage in funny ways: she runs off suitors by making herself look ugly.

- She finally realizes "I am who I am wherever I am." She accepts her destiny. She will marry a young man who sent her a pin with a bird on it. She lets her birds go, freeing caged creatures who want to fly.

Prewriting

Gather

Think about a book I liked and find another book that is similar yet different. Jot notes about the first book. Keep a response journal as I read the new book.

Now it's time for you to practice this strategy. Read the descriptions below. Mark an **X** in front of the book you would choose to compare and contrast with *Catherine, Called Birdy*. Remember that you can compare two books in a number of ways. For example, you could compare books with the same theme, books by the same author, or books with similar main characters. Explain your choice on the lines below. (Several of the books are appropriate, but just choose one.)

1. ____ *Medieval Castle (Inside Story),* **by Fiona MacDonald** An illustrated book with captions that tells about life in and around a medieval castle

2. ____ *Bridge to Terabithia,* **by Katherine Paterson** A tender novel about two young neighbors, Jesse and Leslie, who share a love of running and a secret kingdom in the woods until a tragedy separates them forever

3. ____ *Dealing with Dragons,* **by Patricia C. Wrede** A humorous novel, set in the age of knights and dragons, about a rebellious princess who would rather live with dragons than marry a prince and live as a proper lady

4. ____ *Famous Men of the Middle Ages,* **by John Haaren, A. B. Poland** A resource book containing short biographies of 34 men from across Europe and Asia who shaped history during the Middle Ages

5. ____ *The Ballad of Lucy Whipple,* **by Karen Cushman** A novel about a young girl who moves to California during the Gold Rush of the 1840s and gradually learns to accept her new home

6. ____ *Charlie and the Chocolate Factory,* **by Roald Dahl** A heartwarming and funny story about a boy who visits a famous chocolate factory

7. ____ *Holes,* **by Louis Sachar** A novel about a young boy in a detention camp who bravely and humorously rebels against the cruel warden and eventually discovers his destiny

_____

_____

_____

_____

Prewriting

Gather

Think about a book I liked and find another book that is similar yet different. Jot notes about the first book. Keep a response journal as I read the new book.

Now it's time for you to practice this strategy. One writer chose the book *Holes* to compare with *Catherine, Called Birdy*. Read the writer's response journal below.

My Response Journal for Holes

The book is funny from the start. The first sentence says, "There was no lake at Camp Green Lake." It's sad, too, that the boys are at the detention camp. The main character is Stanley, a poor boy who was accused of stealing some shoes, but he is innocent. He goes to the "camp for bad boys" instead of to jail.

The camp in Texas is tough. It has snakes, scorpions, poisonous lizards, smelly cots, cold showers, a "wreck" room (everything is broken, "even the people"), and mean, sneaky adults.

The warden, wicked and mean, secretly wants to find a treasure in the dry lake. She makes the boys dig holes in the desert to find it.

Stanley doesn't talk much. He's afraid he'll say the wrong thing and make the other boys mad. He thinks a lot and writes to his mom. Stanley figures out the boys are digging holes to find something, "not just to build character."

Zero is Stanley's friend at the camp. Zero is really smart, but he's homeless and can't read. Stanley teaches Zero to read, and Zero digs Stanley's holes. When Zero runs off, Stanley follows and helps him. Then we learn how Stanley's and Zero's ancestors, who lived in Latvia 100 years ago, also had a deal to help each other. Stanley's great-great-grandfather broke his promise, so his family was cursed.

Stanley and Zero's bad luck (symbolized by the holes they dig) changes to good luck. They can't blame Stanley's "no-good-pig-stealing-great-great-grandfather" for their bad luck anymore.

Stanley first feels destiny when the shoes he's accused of stealing show up. Zero had stolen them because he had no shoes.

PrewRiting

Gather

Think about a book I liked and find another book that is similar yet different. Jot notes about the first book. Keep a response journal as I read the new book.

your own writing

Now it's time for you to practice this strategy. Think about two books you have read. Jot down notes about them.

Book 1:

_____

_____

_____

_____

_____

_____

Book 2:

_____

_____

_____

_____

_____

_____

 Now go back to Rachel's work on page 108 in the Student Edition.

Prewriting

Organize
Use my notes and response journal to make a Venn diagram.

Now it's time for you to practice this strategy. Refer to the notes about *Catherine, Called Birdy* on page 54 and the response journal about *Holes* on page 56. Using that information, fill in the Venn diagram below. For these two books, pay special attention to the characters, settings, and how the stories are told.

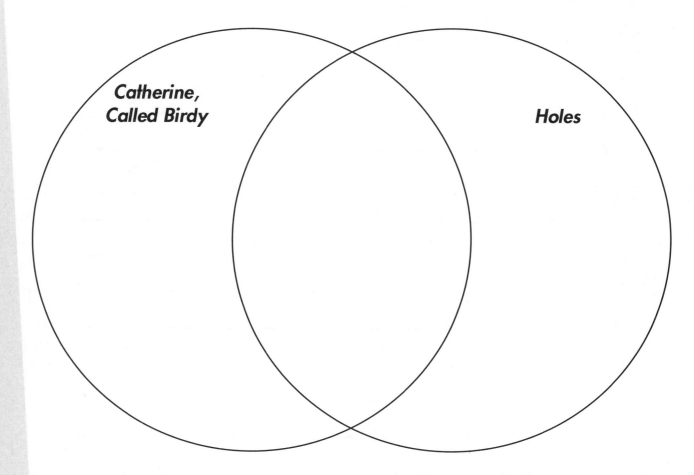

Catherine, Called Birdy

Holes

Prewriting

Organize
Use my notes and response journal to make a Venn diagram.

your own writing

Now it's time for you to practice this strategy. Review your notes on page 57 about the two books that you read. Use your notes to fill in this Venn diagram. Write how each book is the same in the overlapping part of the circles and how each one is different in the rest of each circle.

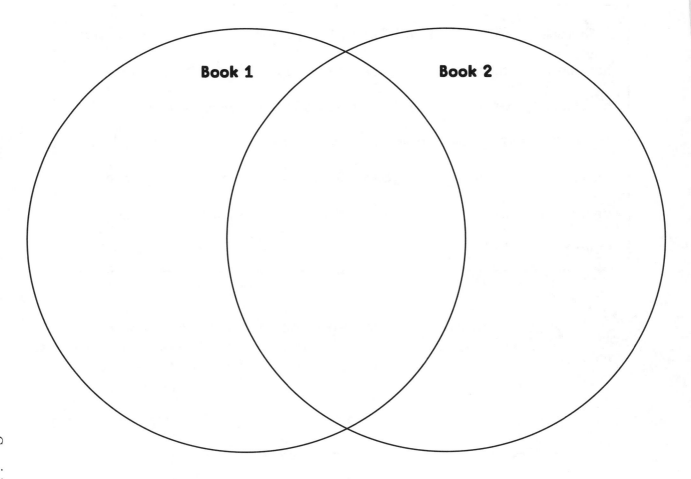

Book 1   Book 2

RETURN
Now go back to Rachel's work on page 110 in the Student Edition.

Drafting

Write
Draft my book review. Start by writing my opinion or thesis statement.

Now it's time for you to practice this strategy. Below is an opening paragraph for a book review about *Catherine, Called Birdy* and *Holes.* Underline the writer's opinion, or thesis statement. A thesis statement can be more than one sentence long.

"Hemming and mending and fishing for husbands" are what the young heroine of Catherine, Called Birdy hopes to avoid. Death by a poisenous lizard, by thirst, or by the warden of the detention camp is what the young hero of Holes hopes to avoid. Catherine, Called Birdy by Karen Cushman shows the struggle young people experience to fulfill there destinies in a world run by adults. Holes by Louis Sachar shows this struggle even better.

your own writing

Now write the opening paragraph for your own review of the two books you chose. Be sure to include a clear thesis statement that states your opinion of the two books. Underline your thesis statement.

_____

_____

_____

_____

_____

RETURN Now go back to Rachel's work on page 112 in the Student Edition.

Persuasive Writing • Book Review

Revising

Elaborate

Check my essay for completeness. Add facts, examples, or quotations to support my comparisons.

Now it's time for you to practice this strategy. Facts, examples, and quotations make your comparisons clearer. The sentences below are based on the notes on page 54 and the response journal on page 56. Place a checkmark in front of the sentences that could help compare the settings of the two books. Remember, the setting is where and when the story takes place.

____ The dried-up lake has snakes, scorpions, and poisonous lizards.

____ Stanley writes letters to his mom.

____ The recreation room is called the wreck room because everything in it is broken, "even the people."

____ Catherine calls her castle a prison.

____ The "camp for bad boys" is in the Texas desert.

____ The cots are smelly and the showers are cold.

____ Stanley eventually realizes they aren't digging holes just to build character.

____ Catherine has to share her bed with fleas and can't bathe all winter because castles in medieval England were very cold.

____ The warden is wicked and mean.

____ The first sentence says, "There was no lake at Camp Green Lake."

____ Part of the story takes place in Latvia 100 years earlier.

____ Catherine teaches Perkin to read.

Remember: Use this strategy in **your own writing**

Now go back to Rachel's work on page 113 in the Student Edition.

ReVising

Clarify
Add signal words to make my comparisons clearer.

Now it's time for you to practice this strategy. These sentences are from one writer's review of *Catherine, Called Birdy* and *Holes*. On the lines, add signal words to make each comparison clearer. You can use signal words from the box or choose your own signal words.

Compare	Contrast
in the same way as	on the other hand
similarly	in contrast (to)
likewise	unlike
like	although
as	however
also	yet
and	but
in addition	nevertheless

1. Both books stress the idea of accepting destiny, _____ the message is stronger in *Holes*.

2. Catherine knows she's supposed to marry a man chosen by her father.

   _____ Catherine, Stanley does not know what his destiny is supposed to be.

3. Stanley is the same age as Catherine. _____, he is not as outspoken.

4. _____ Catherine, Stanley is the victim of a greedy adult.

5. _____ Catherine, Stanley does not complain about his difficult life.

 Now go back to Rachel's work on page 114 in the Student Edition.

Remember: Use this strategy in **your own writing**

Persuasive Writing • Book Review

⌐ Indent.	ℓ Take out something.
≡ Make a capital.	⊙ Add a period.
/ Make a small letter.	⌗ New paragraph
∧ Add something.	SP Spelling error

Editing

Proofread

Check to see that all dependent clauses are part of complex sentences.

Now it's time for you to practice this strategy. Here is part of a book review about *Catherine, Called Birdy* and *Holes*. Use the proofreading marks to correct any errors. Use a dictionary to help with spelling.

Birdy and Stanley—Comparing Two Struggles

"Hemming and mending and fishing for husbands" are what the young heroine of Catherine, Called Birdy hopes to avoid. Death by a poisenous lizard, by thirst, or by the warden of the detention camp is what the young hero of Holes hopes to avoid. Catherine, Called Birdy by Karen Cushman shows the struggle young people experience to fulfill there destinies in a world run by adults. Holes by Louis Sachar shows this struggle even better.

Catherine is fourteen. She describes herself as "stubborn, peevish, and prickly as a thistle." She always speaks her mind. Although she dreams of marriage someday. She protests when she finds out her greedy father is planning to sell her "like a cheese to some lack-wit seeking a wife."

Although Stanley is the same age as Catherine. He is not as outspoken. At the detention camp, he doesn't say much. Because he's afraid he'll make the other boys mad. Like Catherine, he's the victim of a greedy adult— the warden. For years, she has made the boys at the camp dig holes in a dried-up lake. Stanley eventually realizes they aren't digging holes "just to build character." They are looking for something. Unlike Catherine, however, he does not complain about his difficult life. He takes pride in his work, and it makes him stronger.

Remember: Use this strategy in **your own writing**

Now go back to Rachel's work on page 116 in the Student Edition.

Using a Rubric

Use this rubric to evaluate Rachel's book review on pages 117–119 in your Student Edition. You can work with a partner.

Audience

Does the writer clearly express his or her opinion to the reader and support this opinion convincingly?

Organization

Does the writer organize the review so the comparisons are clear?

Elaboration

Does the writer use facts, examples, and quotations to support the comparisons?

Clarification

Does the writer use signal words to make the similarities and differences clear?

your own writing

Save this rubric. Use it to check your own writing.

Conventions & Skills

Does the writer avoid using dependent clauses as sentences?

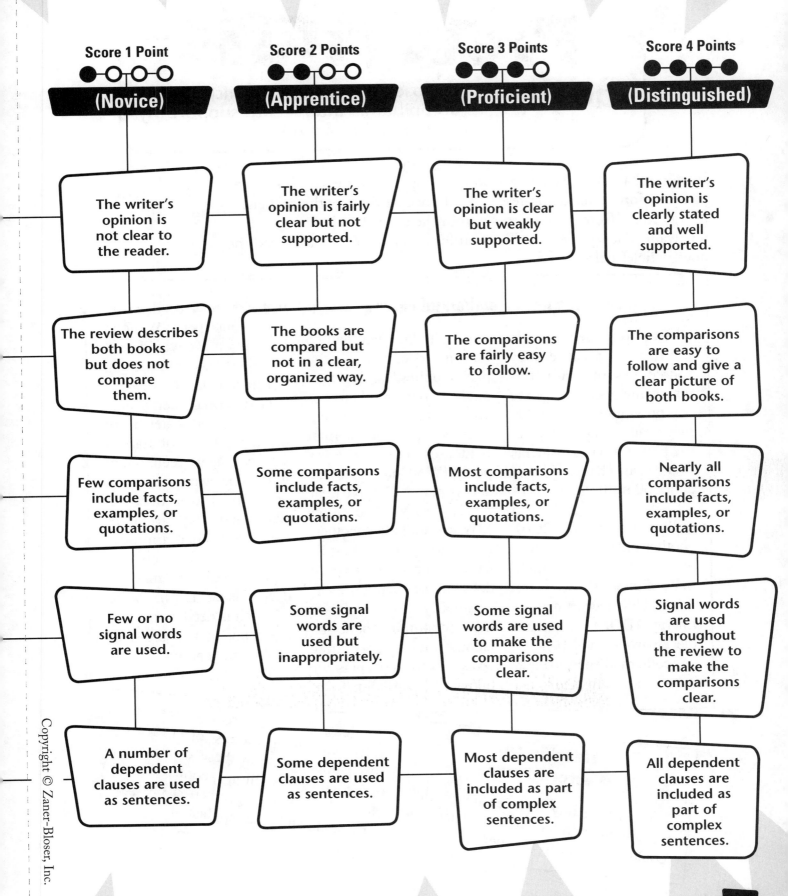

Score 1 Point
(Novice)

Score 2 Points
(Apprentice)

Score 3 Points
(Proficient)

Score 4 Points
(Distinguished)

The writer's opinion is not clear to the reader.

The writer's opinion is fairly clear but not supported.

The writer's opinion is clear but weakly supported.

The writer's opinion is clearly stated and well supported.

The review describes both books but does not compare them.

The books are compared but not in a clear, organized way.

The comparisons are fairly easy to follow.

The comparisons are easy to follow and give a clear picture of both books.

Few comparisons include facts, examples, or quotations.

Some comparisons include facts, examples, or quotations.

Most comparisons include facts, examples, or quotations.

Nearly all comparisons include facts, examples, or quotations.

Few or no signal words are used.

Some signal words are used but inappropriately.

Some signal words are used to make the comparisons clear.

Signal words are used throughout the review to make the comparisons clear.

A number of dependent clauses are used as sentences.

Some dependent clauses are used as sentences.

Most dependent clauses are included as part of complex sentences.

All dependent clauses are included as part of complex sentences.

PrewRiting

Gather

Choose an issue about which I have an opinion. Find facts to support my opinion and take notes.

Imagine that you have decided to write a persuasive essay about energy conservation. After doing research, you decide that geothermal energy, energy made from heat sources within the earth, would be a good renewable energy resource. To get information, you find and read the news articles below.

DOE Supports Geothermal Energy

Heat from deep within Earth is a great energy source. As of 2000, this renewable energy resource was providing almost 3,000 megawatts (MW) of electric power to U.S. residents every year. That is equal to about 60 million barrels of oil, enough energy for 3.5 million homes. By 2010, geothermal sources should be providing about 15,000 MW of energy.

The U.S. Department of Energy (DOE) points out the environmental benefits of geothermal energy. First, it does not burn fuel. That means it does not pollute the air. Also, the average plant requires less land than nuclear power plants or coal plants and their mining operations. A geothermal field uses only 1–8 acres per MW. Coal uses 19 acres per MW. Nuclear power uses 5–10 acres per MW. In addition, geothermal energy uses Earth's natural forces. However, it does not use them up.

Equally important are the economic benefits. Geothermal energy now costs four to eight cents per kilowatt (KW) hour. Soon that cost may be down to three cents per KW hour. In addition, we would need to import less fuel, helping our trade balance.

Geothermal energy uses naturally hot water from the top 50 feet of Earth's surface. New technology will pipe water through hot, dry rocks deep in Earth and draw it up in wells. Another limitless heat source of energy is molten rock, or magma, deep inside Earth. More research is needed to study these potential sources of geothermal energy.

Heating Up Western States

A recent study revealed nearly 300 communities in ten western states that could use nearby geothermal energy resources. These resources are thermal wells with temperatures of at least 50°C. Populations in these communities total 7.4 million people. They would be able to use geothermal energy for heating and other applications.

Prewriting

Gather

Choose an issue about which I have an opinion. Find facts to support my opinion and take notes.

Now it's time for you to practice this strategy. On the lines below, take notes on the articles on page 66.

- Heat from underground provides electricity to U.S. citizens
- Geothermal energy is better for the environment
- Doesn't take much space
- Also it least expensive
- Majority people use it

Prewriting

Gather

Choose an issue about which I have an opinion. Find facts to support my opinion and take notes.

your own writing

Now it's time for you to practice this strategy. Think about another issue about which you have a strong opinion. It could be something related to conserving energy or recycling. Or it might be something related to your school, like whether students should wear uniforms. Locate information on your topic. Use this page to take notes to support your opinion.

-Are video games a lesson for kids in thier future.
-

 Now go back to Anthony's work on page 129 in the Student Edition.

Prewriting

Organize

Use a network tree to organize my ideas.

Now it's time for you to practice this strategy. Use your notes on page 67 to fill in the facts for this network tree.

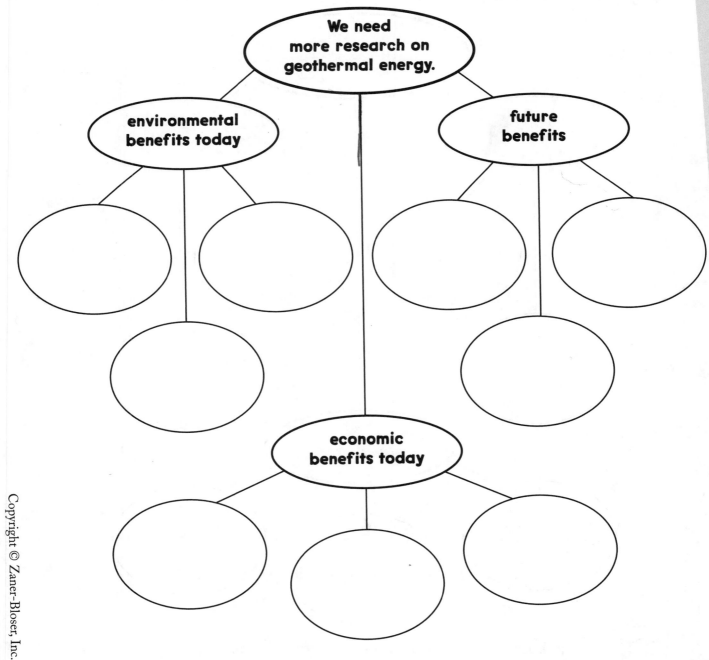

We need more research on geothermal energy.

environmental benefits today

future benefits

economic benefits today

PrewRitiNg

Organize Use a network tree to organize my ideas.

your own writing

Now it's time for you to practice this strategy. Use the network tree below to organize your notes from page 68. Use as much of the network tree as you need.

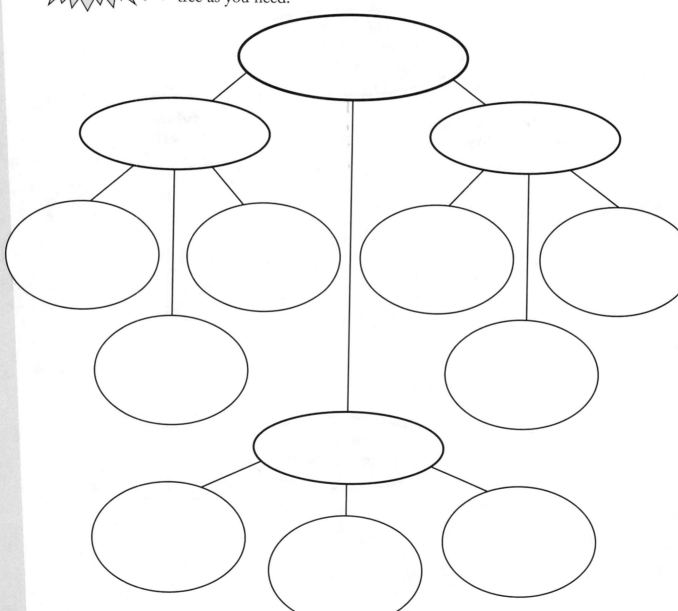

 Now go back to Anthony's work on page 130 in the Student Edition.

Drafting

Write Draft my essay. State my opinion in the first paragraph and support it with reasons and facts in the following paragraphs. Restate my opinion in the last paragraph.

Below is the first paragraph of a persuasive essay on geothermal energy. On the lines below, restate the writer's opinion in your own words.

> Everyone is always whining and wailing about our energy problems. It's all hot air unless we put our money where our future is—in geothermal energy. This energy is available in the hot water, hot rocks, and hot magma inside Earth. Let's not waste more money on coal and nucular power. Instead, let's support research and development in geothermal energy.

_____

_____

_____

Read the facts below. Circle the three that could be used to support the writer's opinion about geothermal energy.

Facts and Reasons

Geothermal plants do not pollute the air.

Magma is also produced by volcanoes.

Geothermal plants require drilling wells.

Geothermal energy is renewable.

Geothermal plants use less land than traditional power plants.

Drafting

Write

Draft my essay. State my opinion in the first paragraph and support it with reasons and facts in the following paragraphs. Restate my opinion in the last paragraph.

your own writing

Now it's time for you to practice this strategy. Use this page and the next page to draft your own persuasive essay about a topic of your choice. Use your notes and your network tree on pages 68 and 70.

_____

_____

_____

_____

_____

_____

_____

_____

_____

_____

_____

_____

_____

_____

_____

_____

_____

Drafting

Write

Draft my essay. State my opinion in the first paragraph and support it with reasons and facts in the following paragraphs. Restate my opinion in the last paragraph.

_____

_____

_____

_____

_____

_____

_____

_____

_____

_____

_____

_____

_____

_____

_____

_____

_____

 Now go back to Anthony's work on page 132 in the Student Edition.

ReVising

Elaborate

Add appropriate and convincing facts or reasons to support my opinion.

Now it's time for you to practice this strategy. Below is a draft of one writer's essay about geothermal energy. Cross out two facts that would not convince readers to support research in geothermal energy. Then add the three facts below. Put them in the essay where you think they should be placed. (Correct any other errors you see now, or wait until later.)

Facts to add:

In fact, geo plants meet the strictest clean-air standards.

Little children in future generations will not have to worry about freezing to death.

You might get a job in this industry and become part of the future of renewable energy.

Fund Research in Geothermal Energy Now!

Everyone is always whining and wailing about energy problems. It's all hot air unless we put our money where our future is—in geothermal energy. This energy is available in the hot water, hot rocks, and hot magma deep within Earth. Let's not waste more money on coal and nucular energy. Instead, let's support research and development in geo energy.

Geo energy is better for Earth than traditional resources. It doesn't burn fuel, so it's clean. It even uses less land. A geo field needs only 1–8 acres per megawatt of energy. Compare that to 19 acres for coal and 5–10 acres for nuclear power. Plus, geo energy is renewable. It doesn't use up Earth's limited fuel resources.

ReVising

Elaborate

Add appropriate and convincing facts or reasons to support my opinion.

Consider the money we can save. Geo energy will soon cost as little as traditional forms of energy. If the United States used more geo energy, we wouldn't have to import as much oil. That would help our world trade balance. Also, the geo industry would provide more jobs at home.

The current geo source is underground hot water. One recent study shows that nearly 300 communities in 10 western states could use thermal wells. Thermal wells have a temperature of at least 50 degrees C. Soon we may be able to pipe water across hot rocks deep inside Earth and then pump them back up to Earth's surface. Communities across the nation could make use of these geothermal sources. However, this needs more research to make it profitable. We may also be able to harnis the heat of magma from deep inside Earth. Magma is called lava when it reaches Earth's surface.

Geo energy is clean, land-efficient, and renewable. It's "homegrown" and becoming as inexpensive as traditional energy. Growth in the industry is promising. Many communities in the West can use current geo energy resources for its heat. What we need is support for new forms of geo energy. Then we may all be blowing renewable hot air in the future.

Remember: Use this strategy in **your own writing**

Now go back to Anthony's work on page 133 in the Student Edition.

RETURN

Persuasive Writing • Persuasive Essay

ReVising

Clarify

Check to see that I have avoided using loaded words.

Now it's time for you to practice this strategy. The paragraphs below are from one writer's essay about geothermal energy. Several loaded words are underlined. On the lines below, rewrite the sentences with loaded words. Replace the loaded words with words that do not unfairly use readers' emotions to sway their opinions.

Fund Research in Geothermal Energy Now!

Everyone is always whining and wailing about energy problems. It's all hot air unless we put our money where our future is—in geo energy. Geo energy is available in the hot water, hot rocks, and hot magma deep within Earth. Let's not waste more money on coal and nuclear energy. Instead, let's support research and development of geo energy.

Geo energy is better for Earth than traditional resources. It doesn't burn fuel, so it's clean. In fact, geo plants meet the strictest clean-air standards. It even uses less land. A geo field needs only 1–8 acres per megawatt of energy. Compare that to 19 acres for coal and 5–10 acres for nuclear power. Plus, geo energy is renewable. It doesn't use up Earth's limited fuel resources. Little children in future generations will not have to worry about freezing to death.

Remember: Use this strategy in **your own writing**

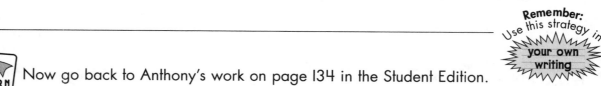

Now go back to Anthony's work on page 134 in the Student Edition.

Editing

Proofread

Check to see that each pronoun has a clear antecedent and that the pronoun and antecedent agree.

Proofreading marks:
- ⊐ Indent.
- ≡ Make a capital.
- / Make a small letter.
- ∧ Add something.
- ℓ Take out something.
- ⊙ Add a period.
- ⌗ New paragraph
- SP Spelling error

Now it's time for you to practice this strategy. Here is part of one writer's draft about geothermal energy. Use the proofreading marks to correct any errors. Pay special attention to pronouns and their antecedents. Use a dictionary to help with spelling.

Growth in the geothermal energy industry is promising. By 2010, the U.S. Department of Engery expects it to produce about five times as much energy as they do now. That would mean you could service about 17 million homes.

The current geo source is underground hot water. One recent study shows that nearly 300 communities in 10 western states could use this kind of geo source. Soon we may be able to pipe water across hot rocks deep inside Earth and then pump them back up to Earth's surface. Communities across the nation could make use of these geothermal sources. However, this needs more research to make it profitable. We may also be able to harnis the heat of magma from deep inside Earth.

Remember:
Use this strategy in
your own writing

RETURN

Now go back to Anthony's work on page 136 in the Student Edition.

Using a Rubric

Use this rubric to score Anthony's persuasive essay on page 137 in your Student Edition. You can work with a partner.

Audience

Does the writer begin by clearly expressing his or her opinion to the audience?

Organization

Does the writer organize the essay so opinions are supported with facts?

Elaboration

Does the writer choose appropriate and convincing facts and reasons to support his or her opinion?

Clarification

Does the writer avoid using loaded words?

Conventions & Skills

Does the writer use pronouns with clear antecedents and make sure that pronouns and their antecedents agree?

your own writing

Save this rubric. Use it to check your own writing.

Score 1 Point	Score 2 Points	Score 3 Points	Score 4 Points
●○●○	●●○○	●●●○	●●●●
(Novice)	**(Apprentice)**	**(Proficient)**	**(Distinguished)**

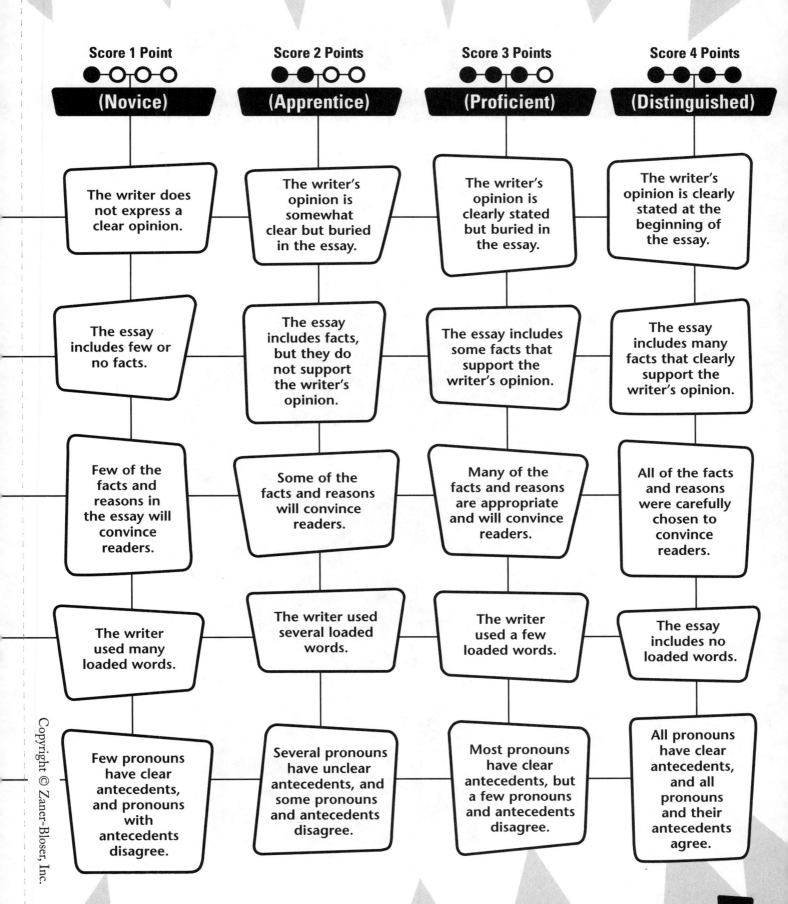

The writer does not express a clear opinion.

The writer's opinion is somewhat clear but buried in the essay.

The writer's opinion is clearly stated but buried in the essay.

The writer's opinion is clearly stated at the beginning of the essay.

The essay includes few or no facts.

The essay includes facts, but they do not support the writer's opinion.

The essay includes some facts that support the writer's opinion.

The essay includes many facts that clearly support the writer's opinion.

Few of the facts and reasons in the essay will convince readers.

Some of the facts and reasons will convince readers.

Many of the facts and reasons are appropriate and will convince readers.

All of the facts and reasons were carefully chosen to convince readers.

The writer used many loaded words.

The writer used several loaded words.

The writer used a few loaded words.

The essay includes no loaded words.

Few pronouns have clear antecedents, and pronouns with antecedents disagree.

Several pronouns have unclear antecedents, and some pronouns and antecedents disagree.

Most pronouns have clear antecedents, but a few pronouns and antecedents disagree.

All pronouns have clear antecedents, and all pronouns and their antecedents agree.

Prewriting

Gather

Choose a picture and take notes about the sensory details in it.

The photograph below shows men placing a capstone on a column. The capstone will crown the tall column. Study the actions and details shown in the picture. On page 81, you will take notes on this picture.

Descriptive Writing • Descriptive Essay

Prewriting

Gather

Choose a picture and take notes about the sensory details in it.

your own writing

Now it's your turn to practice this strategy. On the lines below, take notes about the sensory details in the picture on page 80. You should include what you see and any other senses that might be involved in the picture, such as hearing, smelling, touching, and tasting.

_____

_____

_____

_____

_____

_____

_____

_____

_____

_____

_____

_____

_____

_____

_____

_____

 Now go back to Blue Star's work on page 150 in the Student Edition.

Descriptive Writing • Descriptive Essay

Prewriting

Organize
Use my notes to make a spider map.

your own writing

Now it's time for you to practice this strategy. Using the notes you took on page 81, make a spider map. Group the notes into the categories marked on each "spider leg."

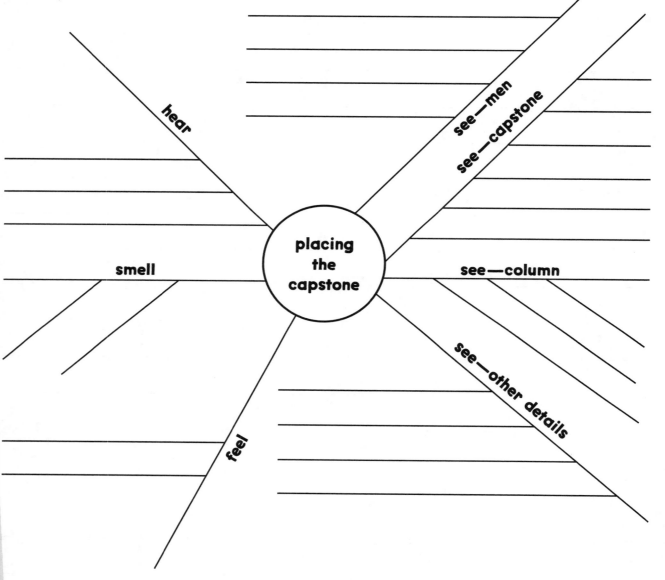

hear

see—men

see—capstone

smell

placing the capstone

see—column

see—other details

feel

 Now go back to Blue Star's work on page 152 in the Student Edition.

Drafting

Write

Draft my essay. Include detail sentences that clearly and vividly describe the picture.

your own writing

Now it's time for you to practice this strategy. Write your own first draft of a descriptive essay about the photograph on page 80. Use your notes on page 81 and spider map on page 82 to help organize the details into paragraphs. Continue your draft on the next page.

_____

_____

_____

_____

_____

_____

_____

_____

_____

_____

_____

_____

_____

_____

_____

_____

_____

DRafting

Write

Draft my essay. Include detail sentences that clearly and vividly describe the picture.

_____

_____

_____

_____

_____

_____

_____

_____

_____

_____

_____

_____

_____

_____

_____

_____

Now go back to Blue Star's work on page 154 in the Student Edition.

Descriptive Writing • Descriptive Essay

ReVising

Elaborate

Add metaphors to help the reader visualize the picture.

Now it's time for you to practice this strategy. In Column A are several topics from the capstone photograph. Add another topic of your choice. In Column B are possible things to compare with the topics in Column A. Add a possible comparison for the topic you added to Column A.

Now draw a line from each topic in Column A to a topic in Column B. Then write a sentence with each metaphor you created on the lines below. Consider using these metaphors in your own descriptive essay.

Column A	Column B
workers	standing giants
capstone	tightrope
tall buildings	circus performers
scaffolding	background music
horns honking	huge scroll
Your topic:	Comparison for your topic:
_____	_____

1. _____

2. _____

3. _____

4. _____

5. _____

6. _____

Remember: Use this strategy in **your own writing**

 Now go back to Blue Star's work on page 155 in the Student Edition.

ReVising

Clarify

Make sure every paragraph has a topic sentence and all the detail sentences relate to that topic.

Now it's time for you to practice this strategy. The paragraphs below are from another writer's draft about the capstone photograph. You will see some errors. The first paragraph has a detail sentence that doesn't belong. Draw a line through that sentence. The second paragraph is missing a topic sentence. Write a topic sentence for that paragraph on the lines below.

The capstone hangs in the middle of the picture. Big as a king-size bed, it will crown the column. It's not only big; it's also beautiful. The capstone is a gigantic, eligant scroll. Carved lines follow its graceful curves and rolls. In the background is a hazy, smoky sky.

The men have only the capstone to hang on to. What if the crane swings the capstone too far in one direction? It might cause the workers to step off the scaffolding. In one corner of the scaffolding is a bucket that they might trip over. In another corner is a hammer and a yardstick.

_____

_____

_____

Remember: Use this strategy in **your own writing**

Now go back to Blue Star's work on page I56 in the Student Edition.

Editing

Proofread   Check to see that I have used appositives correctly.

Now it's time for you to practice this strategy. Here is part of one writer's descriptive essay about the capstone photograph. Use the proofreading marks to correct any errors, especially in punctuating appositives. Use a dictionary to help with spelling.

Skyscrapers do not appear by magic one old black-and-white photograph shows the skill involved in constructing these tall buildings. It is a picture of men placing a capstone the top piece of a column. They are high above a city street. In the distance are blocks of buildings and a water tower. Plumes of foul white smoke sift into the hazey skyline. The sounds of the city, horns honking and people talking are background music to the dramatic scene.

Three construction workers in hats and overalls are positioned at one side of the capstone. Two are at the left corner and one is at the right. They stand on narrow boards in a shakey square of scaffolding. The men are circus performers as they carefully navigate the scaffolding their tightrope. Through the center of the square, the ribbed column rises from the street far below.

Grunting as they labor, the men grip the smooth, curling corners of the capstone and slowly shift it until it is exactly over the column. "A little more this way," one might be saying. "That's it."

 Now go back to Blue Star's work on page 158 in the Student Edition.

Remember: Use this strategy in **your own writing**

Descriptive Writing • Descriptive Essay   **87**

Using a Rubric

Use this rubric to evaluate Blue Star's descriptive essay on page 159 in your Student Edition. You can work with a partner.

Does the writer describe the picture for the reader in a clear, vivid, and interesting way?

Does the writer organize the essay so it flows smoothly?

Does the writer use metaphors to help the audience visualize the picture?

Clarification

Does each paragraph have a topic sentence, supported with detail sentences?

your own writing

Save this rubric. Use it to check your own writing.

Does the writer use appositives correctly to make the description clearer?

Score 1 Point	Score 2 Points	Score 3 Points	Score 4 Points
●○○○	●●○○	●●●○	●●●●
(Novice)	**(Apprentice)**	**(Proficient)**	**(Distinguished)**
The description is confusing and uninteresting.	The description is fairly clear but mostly uninteresting.	The description is clear and fairly interesting, but not especially vivid.	The description is very clear, vivid, and interesting.
The essay is confusing and rambling.	Parts of the essay are organized, but it lacks an overall plan.	Most of the essay is organized, but parts of it do not flow smoothly.	The essay is well organized and flows smoothly.
Either there are no metaphors in the essay, or the metaphors do not make sense.	A few metaphors are included, but they are not well chosen.	Several metaphors are included, but they could be clearer.	All metaphors are well chosen and add to the description.
Few paragraphs have strong topic sentences; many detail sentences are weak or misplaced.	The topic sentences could be stronger; several detail sentences are misplaced.	Many paragraphs have good topic sentences; most detail sentences are in the correct paragraphs.	All paragraphs have good topic sentences; all detail sentences are in the correct paragraphs.
The essay includes no appositives, or they are unclear.	A few appositives are used correctly, but they are not well chosen.	Several appositives are used correctly and help make the description clearer.	Several appositives are used correctly and help bring the description to life.

Prewriting

Gather   Observe and take notes.

Read one writer's notes below. They were taken before, during, and after an experiment about sound vibrations. Then read the directions on the next page.

My Notes on the Sound Vibrations Experiment

- **My question:** Does sound change when you hear it through the bones in your head instead of through the air?

- **My prediction:** Sounds will be different (maybe louder?) when they travel through head bones instead of through the air.

- **What I did:** stretched a 4-inch-long, wide rubber band between a chair arm and my left hand and plucked it with my right index finger; listened to the sound; stretched the same rubber band between my teeth and fingers and plucked it with my finger; listened to sound; repeated the same steps with a 4-inch-long, narrow rubber band.

- **Observations:** Wide rubber band made a "fwap" sound when stretched between chair arm and hand. It made a louder twang when stretched between teeth and fingers. Narrow rubber band made a higher-pitched twang when stretched between chair arm and hand and a higher-pitched and louder twang when stretched between teeth and fingers.

- **Conclusion:** My prediction is correct; sound is louder when it travels through bones. Also, a narrow rubber band makes a higher-pitched sound than a wide rubber band.

Prewriting

Gather   Observe and take notes.

your own writing

Now it's time for you to practice this strategy with a different topic. You will work with a partner to conduct a short experiment on the use of your thumbs. First, read the question below. Then predict the answer to the question.

The question: __What kinds of tasks depend on having thumbs?_____

My prediction: _____

Now take turns taping your thumbs to your hands so you cannot use them. Have your partner help you. Then try to perform several tasks, such as sharpening a pencil, writing your name, buttoning your shirt, and tying your shoelaces. Have one partner take notes on what happens.

Notes:

_____

_____

_____

_____

_____

_____

_____

_____

_____

RETURN   Now go back to Zachary's work on page 169 in the Student Edition.

PrewRiting

Organize

Use my notes to make a sequence chain of the steps in the experiment.

One writer created the sequence chain below, which shows the steps in the sound experiment. It is based on the notes on page 90. Read the sequence chain; then read the directions on the next page.

Step 1: I put a wide rubber band around a chair arm. I pulled it out about 5 inches and plucked it with my other hand. I recorded what it sounded like.

Step 2: I held one end of the same rubber band with my teeth. I pulled it out about 5 inches and plucked it again. I listened and recorded what I heard.

Step 3: I repeated Step 1 with a narrow rubber band.

Step 4: I repeated Step 2 with a narrow rubber band.

Prewriting

Organize

Use my notes to make a sequence chain of the steps in the experiment.

your own writing

Now it's time for you to practice this strategy. Using the notes you took on page 91, make a sequence chain that identifies the steps in your experiment about thumbs. Your first step will probably be taping your thumbs with your partner's help.

Each step might be a different activity, such as trying to write your name or tie your shoe. Write as many steps as you completed, adding more boxes, if necessary. Do not forget to record what happened as you tried each activity.

Step 1:

Step 2:

Step 3:

Step 4:

RETURN Now go back to Zachary's work on page 170 in the Student Edition.

Drafting

Write
Draft my report. Include a short introduction, a description of the steps, observations, and conclusions.

your own writing

Now it's time for you to practice this strategy. On these two pages, write the first draft of your report on the experiment about thumbs. Start by thinking of a title and writing an introduction. Then use the headings shown or change them. Your sequence chain on page 93 will help you describe each step in the procedure. Remember to add your observations and conclusions.

Title of Experiment: _____

Introduction (Include the question you are asking and your prediction of the answer):

_____

_____

_____

_____

_____

PROCEDURE

_____

_____

_____

_____

_____

Drafting

Write

Draft my report. Include a short introduction, a description of the steps, observations, and conclusions.

_____

_____

_____

_____

_____

_____

OBSERVATIONS

_____

_____

_____

_____

_____

CONCLUSION

_____

_____

_____

 Now go back to Zachary's work on page 172 in the Student Edition.

Revising

Elaborate
Add diagrams or charts to complete the description.

Now it's time for you to practice this strategy. On this page is part of one writer's draft about the sound experiment. Read the draft. You will see some errors in it.

Violins and Vibrations

My sister Lee hears violin music through her skull. Shes a violinist. Lees chin rests on the instrument when she plays, so the vibrations pass through her chin and the other bones in Lees head. She says the music sounds different through her bones then when you hear it through air. I could'nt understand what she meant until I did a experiment to learn more about sound vibrations.

I explored the difference between the way we hear sounds when theyre traveling through our head bones and through air. I predicted that the sounds would be louder when they travel through bones than when they travel through air.

First, I listened to the sound made when you pluck a ruber band and the sound travels through the air. Than I held the rubber band in my teeth so the sound would travel through the bones in my head.

PROCEDURE

Step 1: I put one end of a wide rubber band around a chair arm. I pulled it out about 5 inches and plucked it with my other hand. I wrote down what it sounded like in my Observation Log.

Use the space below to draw an Observation Log that could be used for this experiment. The log will have two columns: one for the steps in the experiment and one for observations on what happened during each step. Fill in your Observation Log for Step 1.

Revising

Elaborate
Add diagrams or charts to complete the description.

your own writing

Now it's time for you to practice this strategy. Think about the experiment you conducted on thumbs. On this page, make two diagrams for your experiment, or make a diagram and a chart such as an Observation Log.

Now go back to Zachary's work on page 173 in the Student Edition.

Revising

Clarify

Add time-order words where they are needed.

Now it's time for you to practice this strategy. The paragraphs below are from one writer's observation report about the sound vibrations experiment. You will see some mistakes. Read the time-order phrases in the box. Write each phrase where it is needed in the report.

Time-Order Phrases

In the last part,   In the next step,   In the first step,

OBSERVATIONS

_____ I noticed that the wide rubber band made a "fwap" sound when I stretched it between a chair arm and my hand. Thats when I was hearing the sound travel through the air.

_____ the rubber band made a louder twang when I stretched it between my teeth and my hand. The rubber band made my teeth vibrate, and my teeth made the bones in my head vibrate. I was hearing the sound though my head bones.

_____ of the experiment, I did the same activities with the narrow rubber band. Then I noticed that both sounds from the narrow rubber band were higher than the sounds from the wide rubber band.

Remember: Use this strategy in **your own writing**

RETURN Now go back to Zachary's work on page 174 in the Student Edition.

Descriptive Writing • Observation Report

Editing

Proofread

Check to see that I used apostrophes correctly in possessive nouns and contractions.

⊐ Indent.	ℓ Take out something.
≡ Make a capital.	⊙ Add a period.
/ Make a small letter.	⌗ New paragraph
∧ Add something.	SP Spelling error

Now it's time for you to practice this strategy. Here is the introduction to one writer's report about the sound vibrations experiment. Use the proofreading marks to correct any errors. Use a dictionary to help with spelling.

Violins and Vibrations

My sister Lee hears violin music through her skull. Shes a violinist. Lees chin rests on the instrument when she plays, so the vibrations pass through her chin and the other bones in Lees head. She says the music sounds different through her bones then when you hear it through air. I could'nt understand what she meant until I did a experiment to learn more about sound vibrations.

I explored the difference between the way we hear sounds when theyre traveling through our head bones and through air. I predicted that the sounds would be louder when they travel through bones than when they travel through air.

First, I listened to the sound made when you pluck a ruber band and the sound travels through the air. Than I held the rubber band in my teeth so the sound would travel through the bones in my head.

Remember: Use this strategy in **your own writing**

 Now go back to Zachary's work on page 176 in the Student Edition.

Using a Rubric

Use this rubric to evaluate Zachary's observation report on pages 177–179 in your Student Edition. You can work with a partner.

Audience

Does the writer describe the experiment clearly so the reader can visualize each step?

Organization

Does the writer explain the steps in the order they were completed?

Elaboration

Does the writer include diagrams or charts to complete the description?

Clarification

Does the writer use time-order words to clarify the order of events?

Conventions & Skills

Does the writer use apostrophes correctly in possessive nouns and contractions?

your own writing

Save this rubric. Use it to check your own writing.

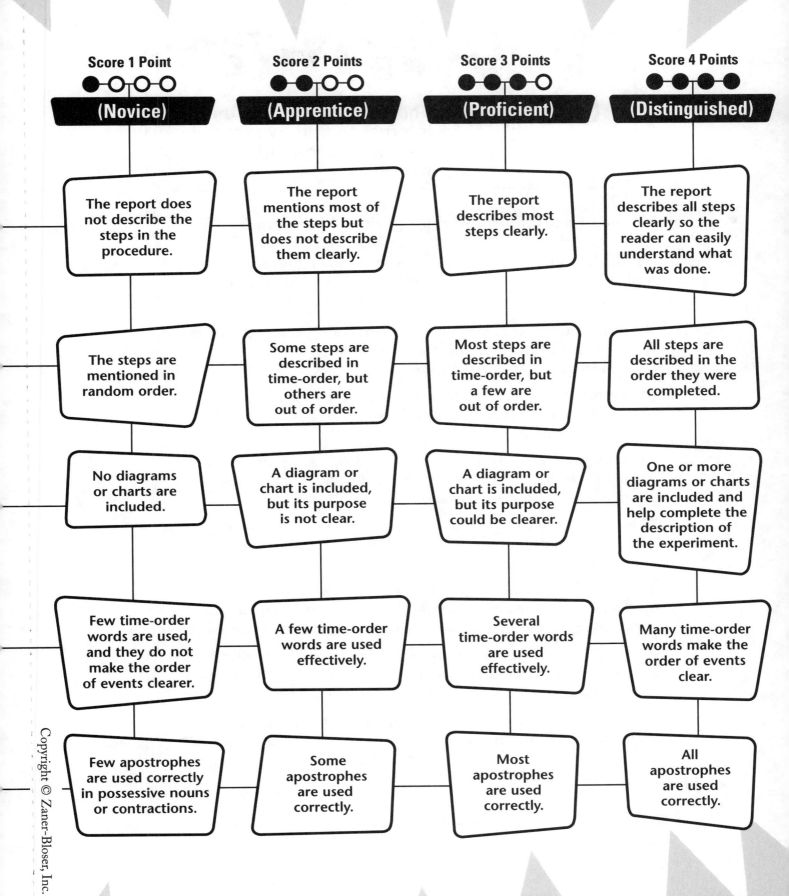

Score 1 Point
●○○○
(Novice)

Score 2 Points
●●○○
(Apprentice)

Score 3 Points
●●●○
(Proficient)

Score 4 Points
●●●●
(Distinguished)

The report does not describe the steps in the procedure.

The report mentions most of the steps but does not describe them clearly.

The report describes most steps clearly.

The report describes all steps clearly so the reader can easily understand what was done.

The steps are mentioned in random order.

Some steps are described in time-order, but others are out of order.

Most steps are described in time-order, but a few are out of order.

All steps are described in the order they were completed.

No diagrams or charts are included.

A diagram or chart is included, but its purpose is not clear.

A diagram or chart is included, but its purpose could be clearer.

One or more diagrams or charts are included and help complete the description of the experiment.

Few time-order words are used, and they do not make the order of events clearer.

A few time-order words are used effectively.

Several time-order words are used effectively.

Many time-order words make the order of events clear.

Few apostrophes are used correctly in possessive nouns or contractions.

Some apostrophes are used correctly.

Most apostrophes are used correctly.

All apostrophes are used correctly.

Prewriting

Gather

Choose my topic. Use the Internet to find two credible sources of information. Take notes.

Now it's your turn to practice this strategy with a different topic. One writer decided to write about why the black-footed ferret is endangered. Here are some possible Internet sources of information for this report. Read each description and put an **X** next to the three sources you would use. Then explain the reasons for your choices.

_____ **Black-footed Ferret** A Web site about the endangered black-footed ferret, created by the U.S. Fish and Wildlife Service. www.endangered.fws.gov/i/a07.html

_____ **My Ferret and Me** A Web site devoted to people who keep ferrets as pets, operated by a teenager named Lily. www.myferretandme.com

_____ **Endangered Species Tees** A Web site for Endangered Species Tees, a company selling T-shirts with pictures of endangered species. www.endangeredspeciestees.com

_____ **"The Road to Recovery: The Black-Footed Ferret"** A recent article by a wildlife biologist in the online magazine _Junior Backpacker_. www.jrbackpacker.com/012/bfferret.htm

_____ **The Fate of the Black-Footed Ferret** An online exhibit, sponsored by Nature Now and Then, a natural history education organization. www.naturenowandthen.org/fate_of_the_black-footed_ferret.html

_____ **_Bart: A Day in the Life of a Black-footed Ferret_, by Dan Larew** A Web site advertising a novel about a black-footed ferret and his struggle to survive. www.backwoodspublishers.com/larewd/bart.html

_____ **"A case study of Montana's reintroduction program for the black-footed ferret"** A master's thesis by a Great Plains College graduate student. www.greatplains.edu/bio/gradmt/davisl.htm

My reasons:

_____

_____

_____

PreWRITiNg

Gather

Choose my topic. Use the Internet to find two credible sources of information. Take notes.

your own writing

Choose your own topic for a cause-and-effect report. Select something that interests you and will interest your classmates. When possible, use the Internet to find at least two credible sources of information for your report. Your teacher or school librarian may be able to help you locate credible sources. List them below and explain the reasons for your choices. Be sure to write down the Web addresses.

Source 1: _____

Web address: _____

My reason for choosing this source: _____

_____

_____

Source 2: _____

Web address: _____

My reason for choosing this source: _____

_____

_____

Now take notes from your sources. Use a separate sheet of paper for each source. Remember to focus on the main ideas.

RETURN Now go back to Carlos's work on page 192 in the Student Edition.

PreWriting

Organize   Make a cause-and-effect chain to organize my notes.

Now it's time for you to practice this strategy. One writer created three cause-and-effect chains with the information she gathered about black-footed ferrets. You can see her chains on these two pages. Which information in the Idea Bank would best fit in each empty box? Make your choices and add that information to the chains.

Idea Bank

Humans killed prairie dogs.

New ferrets were introduced to help build up the population.

Disease spreads faster in captive groups.

Disease and lack of food in the wild remain as problems.

The complete recovery of ferrets is uncertain.

Cause
Humans took over habitat of ferrets and prairie dogs (main food of ferrets).

Cause
Diseases killed prairie dogs and ferrets.

Cause

Effect/Cause
Black-footed ferrets became an endangered species.

Effect/Cause
Humans captured ferrets and bred them in captivity.

Effect

Prewriting

Organize

Make a cause-and-effect chain to organize my notes.

Cause
While ferrets were in captivity, some lost their survival skills.

Cause
High predator populations threaten a small ferret population.

Cause

Effect
Ferrets in the wild are still at risk.

Cause
Captive-breeding programs are expensive to support.

Cause
Inbreeding can occur in captive breeding.

Cause

Effect/Cause
Captive-breeding programs are difficult to manage.

Effect

Remember:
Use this strategy in **your own writing**

PReWRiTiNg

Organize

Make a cause-and-effect chain to organize my notes.

your own writing

Now it's time for you to practice this strategy. Use the boxes on this page and the next page to create a cause-and-effect chain for your report. If you need more than one chain, use another sheet of paper. Remember that a cause can have more than one effect, and an effect can have more than one cause. Change the cause-and-effect chain to fit your information, if necessary.

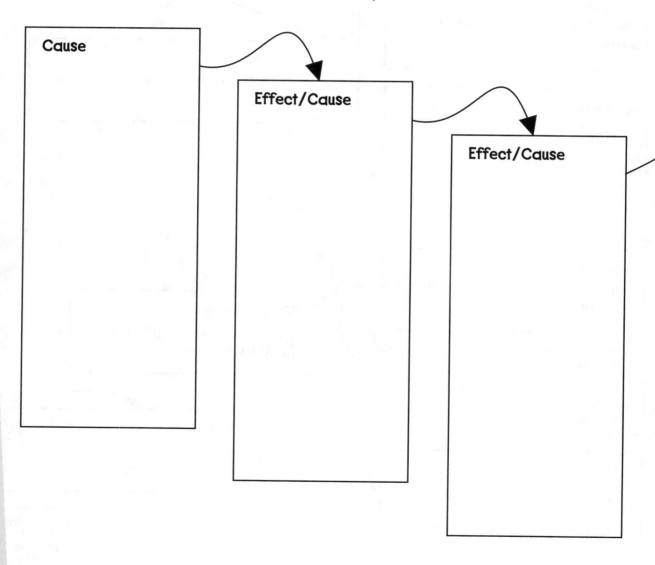

Cause

Effect/Cause

Effect/Cause

Prewriting

Organize

Make a cause-and-effect chain to organize my notes.

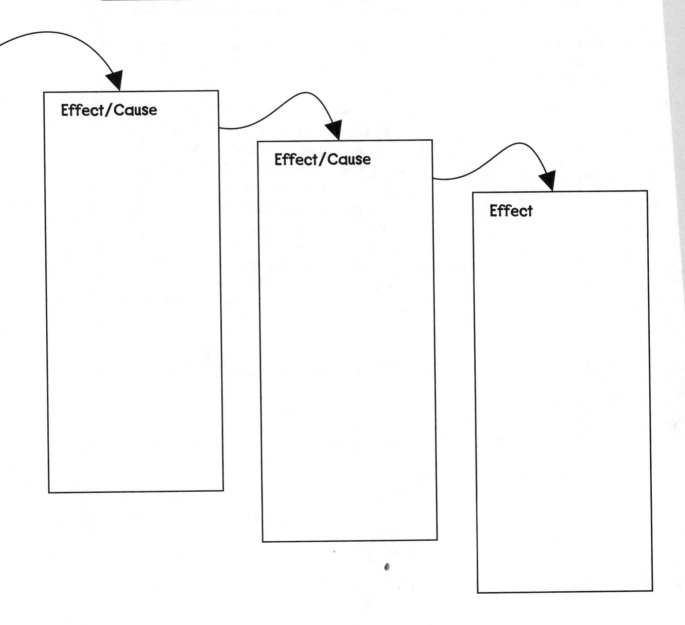

Effect/Cause

Effect/Cause

Effect

RETURN

Now go back to Carlos's work on page 194 in the Student Edition.

Expository Writing • Cause-and-Effect Report

Drafting

Write
Draft my report. Show how each cause leads to an effect.

Here's a paragraph one writer wrote for her report on the black-footed ferret. She used her notes in the cause-and-effect chains on pages 104–105. Read her paragraph.

> Ferrets that are kept in captivity begin to lose their ability to find their own food and protect themselves. When they are released again into the wild, some do not survive. Predators, such as hawks and eagles, are a great threat to the small number of released ferrets. In addition, the released ferrets face disease and lack of food in the wild. For these reasons, ferrets in the wild are still in danger.

Explain the cause and effect in the paragraph above in your own words.

_____

_____

_____

_____

_____

_____

_____

_____

Drafting

Write
Draft my report. Show how each cause leads to an effect.

your own writing

Now it's time for you to practice this strategy. Using your own cause-and-effect chain on pages 106–107, draft your report on the topic you chose. Use this page and the next page. Remember to make the first paragraph as interesting as possible so it will grab your audience's attention. Be sure to show how each cause leads to an effect. Explain each cause and effect in a separate paragraph.

_____

_____

_____

_____

_____

_____

_____

_____

_____

_____

_____

_____

_____

_____

_____

Drafting

Write

Draft my report. Show how each cause leads to an effect.

_____

_____

_____

_____

_____

_____

_____

_____

_____

_____

_____

_____

_____

_____

_____

_____

 Now go back to Carlos's work on page 196 in the Student Edition.

Expository Writing • Cause-and-Effect Report

ReVising

Elaborate Add supporting facts and reasons.

Now it's time for you to practice this strategy. On the left are statements from one writer's report about the black-footed ferret. On the right are facts and reasons. Draw arrows from each statement to the facts and reasons that support it.

Statements

1. Ferrets raised in captivity are in danger of losing their survival skills.

2. Released ferrets still face disease.

3. High predator populations can have a great impact on a released ferret population.

Facts and Reasons

a. Ferrets who are prepared to live in the wild survive at much greater rates than those who aren't.

b. Canine distemper is spread by animals that prey on prairie dog towns, such as coyotes, badgers, and skunks.

c. Coyotes, golden eagles, great-horned owls, prairie falcons, badgers, bobcats, and foxes all hunt the ferret.

d. Diseases carried by prairie dogs are also a threat.

e. Ferrets raised in captivity must be exposed to live prairie dogs and burrows.

f. Canine distemper is always fatal to ferrets.

Remember: Use this strategy in **your own writing**

Now go back to Carlos's work on page 197 in the Student Edition.

ReVising

Clarify

Rewrite sentences that are too long and confusing.

Now it's time for you to practice this strategy. Read the paragraphs below, taken from a report about the ferret. Rewrite them so the sentences are clearer.

> Keeping track of the wild ferret population is hard because ferrets are active only at night, and they live where there aren't many people, and they spend most of their time in underground burrows.
>
> One new reintroduction site is at the Cheyenne River Sioux Reservation where tribal biologists and others who are partners with federal agencies will help count wild ferrets there by checking snow tracks and doing spotlight surveys at night.

_____

_____

_____

_____

_____

_____

Remember: Use this strategy in **your own writing**

 Now go back to Carlos's work on page 198 in the Student Edition.

⌐ Indent.	ℓ Take out something.
≡ Make a capital.	⊙ Add a period.
/ Make a small letter.	⌗ New paragraph
∧ Add something.	ⓈⓅ Spelling error

Proofread

Check to see that subject and object pronouns have been used correctly, especially *who* and *whom*.

Now it's time for you to practice this strategy. Here is part of one writer's draft of the report about ferrets. Use the proofreading marks to correct any errors. Use a dictionary to help with spelling.

By 1980, some thought the black-footed ferret was extinct. Then in 1981 a dog in Wyoming killed a strange animal steeling food from its dish. It looked like a small weasel. It had black feet, a tail tipped with black, and a black mask across its face. The dog's owner took the animal to state wildlife officials, whom identified it as a black-footed ferret.

The excited officials told others, whom went looking for more ferrets. They found a group of they near Meeteetse, Wyoming Several years later, that small colony was nearly wipped out by disease. The last 18 wild ferrets was taken into captivity by scientists, whom believed they could help they breed.

With the help of breeding specialists, the ferrets had young. Now captive breeding populations exist in several states, including Virginia, Colorado, Arizona, and Kentucky. About 200 ferrets live in the wild their young have been born in the wild in three states.

Remember: Use this strategy in **your own writing**

Now go back to Carlos's work on page 200 in the Student Edition.

Using a Rubric

Use this rubric to evaluate Carlos's cause-and-effect report on page 201 in your Student Edition. You can work with a partner.

Audience

Does the writer grab and hold the audience's attention?

Organization

Does the writer organize the report so it follows a cause-and-effect pattern?

Elaboration

Does the writer include supporting facts and reasons?

Clarification

Does the writer avoid using sentences that are too long and confusing?

Conventions & Skills

Does the writer use subject and object pronouns correctly, especially *who* and *whom*?

your own writing

Save this rubric. Use it to check your own writing.

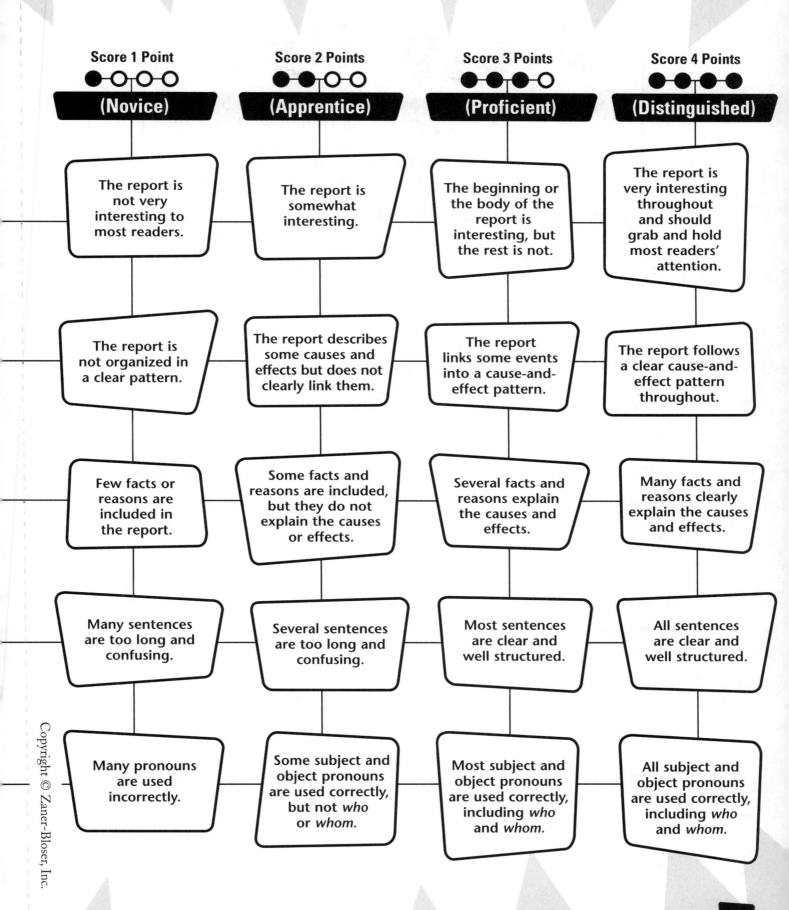

Score 1 Point
● ○ ○ ○
(Novice)

The report is not very interesting to most readers.

The report is not organized in a clear pattern.

Few facts or reasons are included in the report.

Many sentences are too long and confusing.

Many pronouns are used incorrectly.

Score 2 Points
● ● ○ ○
(Apprentice)

The report is somewhat interesting.

The report describes some causes and effects but does not clearly link them.

Some facts and reasons are included, but they do not explain the causes or effects.

Several sentences are too long and confusing.

Some subject and object pronouns are used correctly, but not *who* or *whom.*

Score 3 Points
● ● ● ○
(Proficient)

The beginning or the body of the report is interesting, but the rest is not.

The report links some events into a cause-and-effect pattern.

Several facts and reasons explain the causes and effects.

Most sentences are clear and well structured.

Most subject and object pronouns are used correctly, including *who* and *whom.*

Score 4 Points
● ● ● ●
(Distinguished)

The report is very interesting throughout and should grab and hold most readers' attention.

The report follows a clear cause-and-effect pattern throughout.

Many facts and reasons clearly explain the causes and effects.

All sentences are clear and well structured.

All subject and object pronouns are used correctly, including *who* and *whom.*

Expository Writing • Cause-and-Effect Report

PReWRitiNg

Gather

Choose my topic. Look it up in an encyclopedia to narrow the topic. Check two other sources and make note cards.

Now it's your turn to practice this strategy with a different topic. One writer decided to write a research report on animals. However, when he looked up *animals* in an encyclopedia, he knew right away it was too broad. He had to narrow it down to a more specific topic. Below are two lists of topics. Rewrite each list, putting the topics in order from broad to narrow, as they might be listed in an encyclopedia.

List 1

primates   _____

intelligence of orangutans   _____

animals   _____

animals with backbones   _____

orangutans   _____

List 2

Green Mountains   _____

mountains   _____

Green Mountain National
   Forest   _____

geological formations   _____

mountains in North
   America   _____

mountains in Vermont   _____

Prewriting

Gather

Choose my topic. Look it up in an encyclopedia to narrow the topic. Check two other sources and make note cards.

One writer decided to write a report on the intelligence of orangutans. Read this information he found on a Web site. Then create a note card to record the main points.

Weir, Judith. "Studying the Orangutan." Ape World Magazine. October 2001. www.apeworld.org/orangutan/

Dr. Keith Benton studies intelligence in orangutans. His subjects are young orangutans who live in rain forests on the island of Borneo. Dr. Benton has seen these orangutans make and use tools as they search for food. He has seen them craft seats to make a job more comfortable, create leaf "gloves" to protect their hands, and make leaf "rain hats." His subjects are mainly juveniles, so he believes that older orangutans are probably even more sophisticated.

PrewRitiNg

Gather

Choose my topic. Look it up in an encyclopedia to narrow the topic. Check two other sources and make note cards.

your own writing

Now it's time for you to practice this strategy. Choose a broad topic for a research report and then narrow it down to something more specific. On the lines below, show how you started with a broad topic and used an encyclopedia to narrow it down. List the topics you considered from the broadest one to the narrow one you chose for your report.

_____

_____

_____

_____

_____

Now list two other sources you located and will use in your research report.

1. _____

2. _____

Explain how you selected these two sources.

_____

_____

Now use all the sources you chose to make your note cards.

 RETURN Now go back to Maya's work on page 214 in the Student Edition.

Expository Writing • Research Report

Prewriting

Organize Make an outline to organize my notes.

Now it's time for you to practice this strategy. Read the sentence outline below for the body of a report about orangutan intelligence. The main points are in the box, written as phrases. Decide where each main point would fit in the outline. Write each one there as a sentence, adding necessary words.

learn by imitation	learn language
make and use tools	have self-awareness
use reasoning	

I. _____

    A. Tool-making was once considered unique to humans.

    B. Orangutans rarely use tools in the wild, but they can make and use them.

II. _____

    A. In zoos, they are known as escape artists for their ability to figure out how to get out of captivity.

    B. Experiments prove they use reasoning like humans do.

III. _____

    A. Learning by imitation is an advanced mental ability.

    B. Ex-captive orangutans did things in the wild they had learned by imitating humans.

IV. _____

    A. They have been taught American Sign Language but didn't learn as many words as other types of apes.

    B. Orangutans live alone in the wild, so they may be less likely to "talk" than other apes.

    C. Captive orangutans are being studied to see how they use symbols.

V. _____

    A. Self-awareness is a sign of complex thought.

    B. Orangutans have passed the "mirror" test; they know that the animal in the mirror is themselves.

Prewriting

Organize
Make an outline to organize my notes.

your own writing

Now it's time for you to practice this strategy. Begin writing the outline for the body of your research report below. It should have several main points, each with supporting details. Continue your outline on another sheet of paper, if necessary.

_____

_____

_____

_____

_____

_____

_____

_____

_____

_____

_____

_____

_____

_____

 RETURN Now go back to Maya's work on page 216 in the Student Edition.

Expository Writing • Research Report

Drafting

Write
Draft the body of my report. Write at least one paragraph for every main point on my outline.

Now it's time for you to practice this strategy. Read the paragraphs below from one writer's draft of a report on orangutan intelligence. (Because it's a draft, you will see some mistakes.) Each paragraph supports a main point on the outline on page 119. Beside each paragraph, write the Roman numeral of the main point it supports.

Orangutans are known by zookeepers as escape artists. ~~When they~~ Their ability to figure out how to get out of captivity proves they can problem-solve. One orangutan, Jonathan, has escaped from many zoos. In one zoo he pulled up a tree and set it against an outside wall and crawled out of the exibit. ~~He used~~ In another escape, he set a rubber tire over an electric fence and walked across the tire to freedom. He even used hay to stop a security door from closing all the way. Fu Manchu, another orangutan, got away by picking a lock with a bent wire when the keepers weren't looking. ~~The wire~~ He hid the wire inside his cheek!

_____

Self-awareness is another way to tell if an animal ~~is~~ has high intelligence. Its a sign of complex thought. Orangutans ~~saw~~ have shown that they have self-awareness by passing the "mirror" test. Most animals think they're seeing another animal when they see their reflection in a mirror. Orangutans ~~are able~~ recognize themselves.

_____

Expository Writing • Research Report

Drafting

Write

Draft the body of my report. Write at least one paragraph for every main point on my outline.

your own writing

Now it's time for you to practice this strategy. Choose two main points from your outline on page 120. Then write one or two paragraphs for each main point as part of the first draft of your research report. You will include your main points and supporting details. You can use this page and the next page.

_____

_____

_____

_____

_____

_____

_____

_____

_____

_____

_____

_____

_____

Drafting

Write

Draft the body of my report. Write at least one paragraph for every main point on my outline.

_____
_____
_____
_____
_____
_____
_____
_____
_____
_____
_____
_____
_____
_____
_____

Now go back to Maya's work on page 218 in the Student Edition.

ReVising

Elaborate

Add an introduction that states the topic and interests the reader. Add a conclusion that summarizes the main points.

Now it's time for you to practice this strategy. Below are three introductions for the report on orangutan intelligence. Read them and decide which one is best. Explain the reasons for your decision on the lines.

Introduction 1

"Monkey see, monkey do." Have you ever heard that saying? Do monkeys just imitate what they see or can they figure things out on their own? I decided to study the intelligence of an animal that is closely related to monkeys: orangutans.

Introduction 2

An orangutan is a type of ape. The other types of ape are chimpanzees, gorillas, and gibbons. Like them, orangutans have no tails and are mostly vegetarians. They have a well-developed social structure and human-like intelligence.

Introduction 3

Orangutans live only on two islands: Borneo and Sumatra. They spend most of their time in trees and seldom set foot on the ground. Orangutans are endangered. It is illegal to kill, own, or export them, but people continue to do so. People are also destroying their habitat. If we do not protect the orangutans, they may soon become extinct.

_____

_____

_____

_____

_____

_____

Remember:
Use this strategy in
your own writing

ReVising

Elaborate

Add an introduction that states the topic and interests the reader. Add a conclusion that summarizes the main points.

Now read the three conclusions below. Decide which one is best for a report on orangutan intelligence. Explain the reasons for your decision on the lines.

Conclusion 1

Self-awareness is another indicator of high intelligence. It's a sign of complex thought. Orangutans have shown that they have self-awareness by passing the "mirror" test. Most animals think they are seeing another animal when they see their reflection in a mirror. Orangutans recognize themselves.

Conclusion 2

Orangutans show human-like intelligence. They make and use tools, solve problems by reasoning, learn by imitating, use language, and have self-awareness. Unlike humans, though, orangutans are endangered. Scientists think they are going to be extinct in the wild by 2020. We must save these rare animals.

Conclusion 3

Orangutans are much like humans. They make and use tools, solve problems by reasoning, learn by imitating, use language, and have self-awareness. As scientists continue to study orangutan intelligence, they may also understand human intelligence better.

_____

_____

_____

_____

_____

_____

Remember: Use this strategy in **your own writing**

RETURN Now go back to Maya's work on page 219 in the Student Edition.

ReVising

Clarify   Use active voice as much as possible.

Now it's time for you to practice this strategy. The sentences below are from one writer's report on orangutan intelligence. They are all in passive voice. Rewrite them in active voice.

1. Orangutans are known by zookeepers as escape artists.

_____

2. The camp paths were swept and weeded by orangutans.

_____

3. American Sign Language has been learned by orangutans.

_____

4. One orangutan was taught by its trainer to make stone tools.

_____

5. Orangutans have been seen by researchers using sticks to scratch their backs.

_____

6. Some orangutans from zoos have been released into the wild by researchers.

_____

7. Firewood has been chopped by orangutans after watching humans do it.

_____

8. Orangutans are being observed by scientists to figure out how they learn.

_____

Remember: Use this strategy in **your own writing**

RETURN Now go back to Maya's work on page 220 in the Student Edition.

Editing

⌐ Indent.	ℓ Take out something.
≡ Make a capital.	⊙ Add a period.
/ Make a small letter.	# New paragraph
∧ Add something.	SP Spelling error

Proofread

Check to see that I have correctly capitalized and punctuated proper nouns and proper adjectives.

Now it's time for you to practice this strategy. Here is part of the research report on orangutan intelligence. Use the proofreading marks to correct any errors, especially mistakes in using proper nouns and proper adjectives. Use a dictionary to help with spelling.

Orangutans are also able to learn language that humans can understand. Dr Gary shapiro taught american Sign Language (ASL) to orangutans in the wild. ASL consists of hand gestures. A young female learned about 40 signs for words in Asl, such as **food** and **hug**. Researchers have taught chimpanzees and gorilas hundreds of words.

Orangutans may be able to learn more words, but they live alone in the wild. For that reason, they may be less talkative than other types of Apes. The Orangutan language Project tests the language skills of captive orangutans. It focuses on how they use abstract simbols. The project operates at the National zoo in Washington, dc. Orangutans learn to connect an object, an action, or a quantity of objects with a symbol. researchers think the orangutans may be able to put the symbols in order to communicate ideas.

Remember: Use this strategy in **your own writing**

RETURN Now go back to Maya's work on page 222 in the Student Edition.

Expository Writing • Research Report

I27

Using a Rubric

Use this rubric to evaluate Maya's research report on pages 223–225 in your Student Edition. You can work with a partner.

Audience

Does the writer present the audience with interesting information about a specific topic?

Organization

Does the writer organize the body of the report by writing one or more paragraphs about each main point?

Elaboration

Does the writer add to the report by including an introduction that states the topic in an interesting way and a conclusion that summarizes the main points?

Clarification

Does the writer use the active voice whenever possible?

your own writing

Save this rubric. Use it to check your own writing.

Conventions & Skills

Does the writer correctly capitalize and punctuate proper nouns and proper adjectives?

Score 1 Point
(Novice)

The topic is too broad, and the information is uninteresting.

Several main points are grouped into the same paragraph.

The introduction does not state the topic. The conclusion is unclear or missing.

Most sentences are in passive voice.

Few proper nouns or proper adjectives are correctly capitalized or punctuated.

Score 2 Points
(Apprentice)

The topic is fairly specific, but most of the information is uninteresting.

Some main points are grouped into the same paragraph.

The introduction states the topic but is not interesting. The conclusion does not summarize the main points.

The writer sometimes uses active voice.

Some proper nouns and proper adjectives are correctly capitalized and punctuated.

Score 3 Points
(Proficient)

The topic is specific, but some of the information is uninteresting.

Most main points are discussed in separate paragraphs.

The introduction states the topic and is interesting. The conclusion mentions a few of the main points.

The writer often uses active voice.

Most proper nouns and proper adjectives are correctly capitalized and punctuated.

Score 4 Points
(Distinguished)

The topic is specific, and all of the information is interesting.

All main points are discussed in separate paragraphs.

The introduction states the topic and is interesting. The conclusion clearly summarizes the main points.

The writer uses active voice whenever possible.

All proper nouns and proper adjectives are correctly capitalized and punctuated.

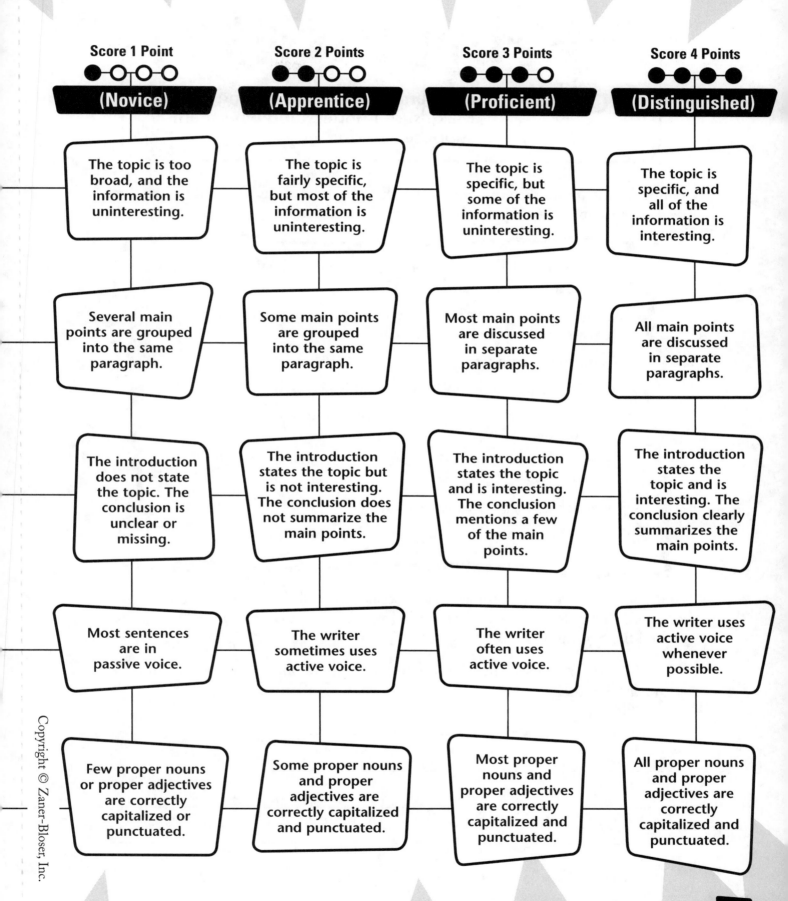

PreWriting

Gather

Read and analyze the writing prompt. Make sure I understand what I am supposed to do.

Now it's time to practice this strategy with a different topic. Carefully read the prompt below. Think about what it asks you to do.

Suppose you had a chance to become very famous. Would you really like to be a famous person?

Explain whether you would or would not like to be a celebrity, and give reasons to support your decision.

Be sure your writing

- clearly identifies the topic for your audience early in the paper.

- is well organized. You should include an introduction, body, and conclusion.

- includes details or facts that help readers understand each main idea.

- uses signal words to connect ideas.

- uses the conventions of language and spelling correctly.

Underline the part of the prompt that describes the task. Then circle the key word that tells you the kind of writing you need to do. Draw a box around the Scoring Guide.

your own writing

Describe what the test asks you to do. Use your own words.

_____

_____

_____

_____

 Now go back to Amber's work on page 238 in the Student Edition.

PreWRiting
Gather & Organize

Choose a graphic organizer. Use it to organize my ideas.
Check my graphic organizer against the Scoring Guide.

your own
writing

Now it's time for you to practice these strategies. Reread the writing prompt on page 130. Then fill in the spider map to plan your explanation of whether you would like to be famous and your reasons why. Add more legs or detail lines if you need them.

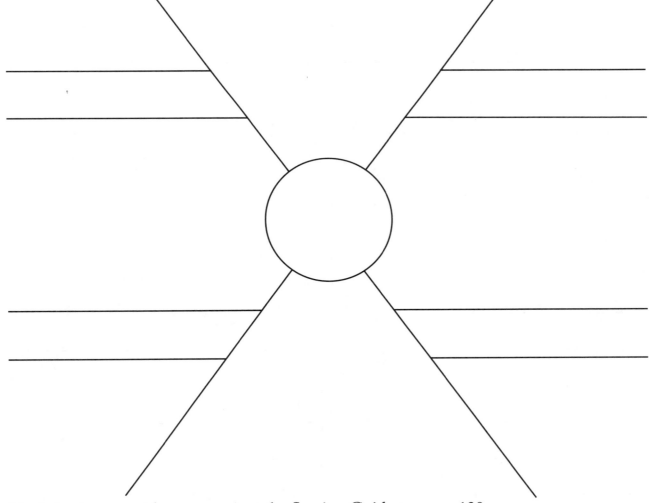

Now check your spider map against the Scoring Guide on page 130.
Make any changes that you think will improve your explanation.

 RETURN Now go back to Amber's work on page 242 in the Student Edition.

Drafting

Write

Use my spider map to write an explanation with a good introduction, body, and conclusion.

your own writing

Now it's your turn to practice this strategy. Refer to your spider map on page 131 as you draft your explanation on this page and the next page. Include an introduction that clearly identifies your topic, a body that explains your reasons, and a conclusion that summarizes your main points or wraps up your ideas.

_____

_____

_____

_____

_____

_____

_____

_____

_____

_____

_____

_____

_____

_____

Drafting

Write

Use my spider map to write an explanation with a good introduction, body, and conclusion.

_____

_____

_____

_____

_____

_____

_____

_____

_____

_____

_____

_____

_____

_____

Now go back to Amber's work on page 244 in the Student Edition.

Test Writing 133

Revising

Elaborate

Check what I have written against the Scoring Guide. Add any missing facts or details.

Now it's time for you to practice this strategy. The paragraph below is part of a draft response to the writing prompt on page 130. Rewrite the paragraph. Add two or more sentences with details or facts that help explain each main idea. Make up the details if you wish.

> One reason I would not want to be famous is that I like to do things on the spur of the moment. If I were famous, I would probably have a whole group of assistants around me all the time.

_____

_____

_____

_____

_____

_____

_____

_____

Remember: Use this strategy in **your own writing**

Now go back to Amber's work on page 245 in the Student Edition.

ReVising

Clarify

Check what I have written against the Scoring Guide. Make sure I have used signal words so that everything is clear.

Now it's your turn to practice this strategy. The writer of the following paragraphs needs to add some signal words to connect ideas. At each place where you see a ^, write in signal words from the Word Bank that will help clarify and connect the ideas. This is a draft, so you will see some errors.

Word Bank

In addition,	The second
As my third reason,	Worst of all,
For example,	As a result,

~~Another~~ reason I would not want to be famous is that my friends
^
and me like to do things on the spur of the moment. If I were famous, I

would probably have a whole group of assistants around me all the time.

I might have a hairdresser, a trainer, and a manager. I would be busy with
^   ^
agents, photographers, and reporters. I would not be able to do any-
                        ^
thing just for fun I would hate that.

   I would not want to be a celebrity because I do not like having people
^
gossip about me. Much of what is said about celebrities is not even true!
                 ^

Remember:
Use this strategy in
**your own
writing**

Now go back to Amber's work on page 246 in the Student Edition.

Editing

⊐ Indent.	ℓ Take out something.
≡ Make a capital.	⊙ Add a period.
/ Make a small letter.	♯ New paragraph
∧ Add something.	SP Spelling error

Proofread

Check that I have used correct grammar, capitalization, punctuation, and spelling.

Now it's time for you to practice this strategy. Below is a revised explanation about why the writer would not want to be a celebrity. Use the proofreading marks to correct any errors in grammar, capitalization, punctuation, and spelling. Add transition words where you see a ∧.

It seems as if it would be fun to be a famous

person celebrity but that is not the lifestyle for me I

would choose.

Their are several reasons why I would not want to

be famous. First of all, Im pretty shy. If I were

famous, I would have to appear at movie openings

and on late knight talk shows. I would probably say

something foolish and embarrass myself. I turn read

when that happens. I think people whom are outgo-

ing enjoy being famous more than those of us whom

are quiet.

~~Another~~ reason I would not want to be famous is

∧ that my friends and me like to do things on the spur

of the moment. If I were famous, I would probably

Editing

⌐ Indent.		ℓ Take out something.	
≡ Make a capital.		⊙ Add a period.	
/ Make a small letter.		# New paragraph	
∧ Add something.		SP Spelling error	

Proofread

Check that I have used correct grammar, capitalization, punctuation, and spelling.

have a whole group of assistants around me all the

time. I might have a hairdresser, a trainer, and a
          ∧
manager. I would be busy with agents, photogra-
          ∧
phers, and reporters. I would not be able to do
          ∧
anything just for fun I would hate that.

    ∧ I would not want to be a celebrity because I do

not like having people gossip about me. Much of what
                              ∧
is said about celebrities is not even true! Just look at

a magazine next time you are in the checkout line at the

grocery store you will see what I mean.

    I like quiet, privacy, and spontaneity. With

these traits, I would make a terrible celebrity.

Remember:
Use this strategy in
your own writing

Now go back to page 249 in the Student Edition.

Using a Rubric

This rubric for expository writing was developed from the Scoring Guide on page 229 in the Student Edition.

Audience

Does the writer clearly identify the topic for the audience early in the paper?

Organization

Is the paper well organized, including an introduction, body, and conclusion?

Elaboration

Does the writer include details or facts that help readers understand each main idea?

Clarification

Does the writer use signal words to connect ideas?

your own writing

Save this rubric. Use it to check your own writing.

Conventions & Skills

Does the writer use the conventions of language and spelling correctly?

Score 1 Point	Score 2 Points	Score 3 Points	Score 4 Points
(Novice)	**(Apprentice)**	**(Proficient)**	**(Distinguished)**
The topic is not clear to the audience throughout the paper.	Several topics are mentioned, but it's not clear which is the main one.	The topic is not clear until the end of the paper.	The topic is clearly identified for the audience in the opening paragraph.
The explanation rambles and is not organized into an introduction, body, and conclusion.	The explanation is missing the introduction and the conclusion.	The explanation is missing the introduction or the conclusion.	The explanation is well organized and includes an introduction, body, and conclusion.
The explanation includes few details or facts to support the main ideas.	The explanation includes some details or facts.	The explanation includes many details or facts, but they are not always linked to the main ideas.	The explanation includes many details or facts that help readers understand the main ideas.
The explanation includes few or no signal words.	The explanation includes a few signal words, but they are not used effectively.	The explanation includes several signal words, but some are not used effectively.	The explanation includes many appropriate signal words to connect ideas in logical ways.
The explanation has many errors in language use and spelling.	The explanation has several errors in language use and spelling.	The explanation has a few errors in language use and spelling.	The explanation has no errors in language use or spelling.